# GAMALIEL
## Beyond the Veil

### Charles G. Dorsey

PRAIRIE MUSE BOOKS INC
2023

## Also by
## Charles G. Dorsey

**NOT ALONE**
*The Birth That Changed The World*

This is a work of fiction. Names, characters, places, and incidents either are the product of the author's imagination or are used fictitiously.

GAMALIEL
Copyright © 2023 by Charles G. Dorsey
Paperback Edition
ISBN: 978-1-952911-50-7

All rights reserved. This book or any portion thereof may not be reproduced or used in any manner whatsoever without the express written permission of the publisher except for the use of brief quotations in a book review.

Prairie Muse Publishing
Lincoln, Nebraska 68520

*Cover Painting by* MIKE ULRICH

# FOREWORD

Growing up in a small town in northeastern Iowa and raised in a Christian home gave me a start of love for the Bible, Jesus, and a fascination about the people who lived at the time before Jesus came to walk in this world. Being a creature of imagination, I was always wondering about what people who were living at that time were thinking.

The Jesus we now know had not yet been presented to the world. The Hebrew nation was led by priests who were locked into the law as given to Moses by Jehovah on Mount Sinai. There had been many interpretations of these laws over the years and added to the original script. Through these, and because of the nation of Israel being under non-godly control of other larger, more powerful governments, it was difficult to remain true to the original Mosaic Law. The priests became more self-purposed on survival under the prevailing government, and the people were moving to survive any way they could. The result was the watering down and lessening of the true worship of Jehovah, God.

Jehovah is always faithful, and through history has always had the seed of His love carried on by one or a few called a "Remnant". This is a story of one early Pharisee who loved and listened to Jehovah and worked to restore the love of Jehovah back into the laws of the Hebrew nation and the passing of that seed of knowledge through his great-grandson who was named Gamaliel.

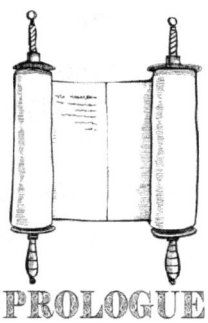

## PROLOGUE

### The Thought Begins

As the four friends stepped over and around the stones of the path that was called a road, they conversed about the time they had just spent together. They were returning from the burial of a distant family member. The passing of the head of this family had also brought about the passing of the family business to the eldest son to carry on in the tradition of many generations. As Hillel moved around a particularly large boulder, he decided to share his thoughts of something new with the others.

"Friends," he began, "I have been thinking about the "Anointed One" Jehovah has said He would send to restore Israel to Himself. What if Jehovah sent his own son, as a father would send his own son, to complete the work he had begun?"

Simeon, a Levite, stopped in the road and just stared at Hillel the Elder. "I have never even considered a thought like that. What did you find in your study to start your thinking in this way? You have always been a great student of the Mosaic Law, but I have never heard you say anything in this manner before."

Hillel looked back at his friend and said, "The thought came to me suddenly while meditating over the loss to the family and the passing of the responsibility of the father to the son. It becomes the son's responsibility to complete the work his father had begun and planned. Jehovah spoke of His son in the old writings and this would fit in the way we have been given to serve Jehovah."

"Does Jehovah actually say this, or have you found it in some small way that you are now bringing for us to add to our thoughts and teachings?" This from Jaddus, who as a priest served in the regular rotation of priestly duties in the temple in Jerusalem, and had become a close friend of Hillel.

"Tell us where you found this," added Jacob, a longtime friend and also a distant relative of the family they had just left. "We would also learn from your findings."

"The idea just appeared in my head, but I believe Jehovah gave it to me. I will study it further, but the more I dwell on it, the more I am coming to believe it to be true," said Hillel as he turned to move down the side of the hill.

# PART I

Just about two thousand years ago, when the Roman government ruled most of the known world, men began thinking about building a system of dating that would keep all countries of the Roman Empire on the same day schedule. The gathering of information was a huge task, and communication was done only by foot and horseback. The work of putting all the gathered information together took seven to ten years before it was organized and complete. Then another period of time passed while gaining acceptance of all peoples who would be affected by the new way of looking at time and seasons.

In the world at this particular time, governments of men ruled by size and power. The more power, the more land area was under the control of the throne of leadership. Leadership was held in control by loyalty of friends, and when that loyalty faded or failed, so did the leadership. Many times the entire government collapsed to be fought over by others who desired the power they thought it would give them in their dealings with subordinate peoples. This was exemplified by the Roman government which at this time governed most of the known world. Human life was not held in high esteem, except for those in charge, and the powerful army of Roman soldiers kept total control or were themselves punished severely. Using this concept of rule, the Roman government was able to expand its authority to cover almost all of the lands known at that time.

One aspect of their rule, the Romans found, was that they could allow a limited amount of localized self-government in these smaller countries to exist—as long as it did not conflict with the Roman laws, and as long as taxes were paid. Taxes were high, but most of the lesser governments could comply and did survive, even in this half slavery situation. There was, of course, protection by the Romans from attempts at invasion by foreign governments trying to gain land area within the sphere of Roman control. These attempts were quickly and brutally quelled by the massive armies of the Roman government moving quickly over the extensive system of roads they had built for that purpose. Many times this resulted in more land being taken and placed under Roman control.

One of these smaller countries under Roman domination was called Israel and was located at the eastern end of the Mediterranean Sea called the "Great Sea". This small country was one of the central land areas through which several ancient trade routes passed. Because of its location and exposure to people from other parts of the world, the people of this small nation-state had been overtaken and ruled by many other nations over the 1000-plus years of their existence. Persians, Syrians, Babylonians, and others sought to dominate Israel. But somehow, through every one of the times of their overlords, these Israelis, who were also known as Hebrews, had been able to maintain their particular identity and strove to return to their homeland—even when many of them had been taken to other lands to endure slavery. Their cry of "Next Year, in Jerusalem" was a call to remembrance that has been heard through many centuries.

The city of Jerusalem was the capital of that small, beloved land, and is still considered so to this day. The history of that land and people was handed down from generation to generation and stored in the mind of each citizen who was then entrusted with keeping the story of the beginning of Israel alive.

The story of Israel was made up of historical people, the facts memorized by all, and in every conversation there was at least one comment by one or another of those present of that history and the laws of Jehovah by which the nation was to be guided. The history and laws had been handed down from Moses who received them from Jehovah, the God not only of Israel, but also of the entire universe. Discussions of the law and history were long and deep and often aroused differences spoken of by one, both, or all the members present. When at last they came to a place of stopping their discussion and going home, it was with acceptance of the fact that they would most likely be back the next day going over the same, or perhaps a different part of the law. This was a favorite aspect of the way of life for the Hebrew people.

For this verbal repetition of the people's history and law to continue, the family was vitally important. Women were married young by arrangement of their fathers, and were expected to bear children in abundance—a son first, but others as Jehovah blessed the couple. The sons were sent to school when young to sit under the training of the local Rabbi, while the daughters were educated in the homes by the mothers. At mealtimes in the home, the Law was a normal part of the conversation with the training of the children being the focus.

One of the most important relationships in the families of this nation was the one between a grandfather and grandson. That relationship was and always has been special, and one of the most cherished learning relationships in history. Because the grandfathers had lived long and gained much wisdom from life, the sharing of that wisdom from the older to the younger was a time-honored part of a boy's life.

As the nation of Israel was forming, a group of men who studied the laws given by Jehovah joined themselves together for the purpose of maintaining the study and understanding of the Mosaic Law as was given to Moses by Jehovah on Mount Sinai. This group came to be known as *Sadducees*.

Many years later, another group of thoughtful men joined together with a different focus drawn from this same law, and the two parties sometimes clashed. But at the same time, they could often work together to guide the nation in what they felt was the proper way to follow and serve their God, Jehovah. This second group of men were known as *Pharisees*.

These Pharisees revered the law as written by Moses, but tried to keep Jehovah in His proper place at the center of all law. The Pharisees also added their own interpretations and insights which when expanded, affected how the people heard and followed the laws. The major difference between these two groups was the belief in life after death. The Pharisees believed there was life after death and the Sadducees did not.

The two groups would debate this subject any time, any place, and for many hours. When the time came to cease for the day, they would part with the knowledge that they would be back the next day debating the same positions as before. Almost all of the major decisions pertaining to the nation were centered here in these two groups.

There were also other groups adding to the mix of beliefs held by the Hebrews at this time. There were *scribes*, whose job it was to keep all records, copy scripture, and ensure that all writings were correct. The scribes, because of their time spent in the scriptures, thought they knew better than the others the proper way to interpret the scriptures. They actually had little input into the lawmaking work of the nation.

There were also *Essenes*, who thought separation from the others and private study of the law was the only way, and many of this group went to live in enclaves away from the clamor of cities and large groups of people.

*Zealots*, a more radical group, were focused on the emotional side of their beliefs and felt that violence was the best way to drive the Romans from their land.

There was, in addition, a small group of *Hellenists*, who were suspended between the beliefs of their ancient Greek gods and their conversion to the worship of Jehovah. All had similar basic beliefs but differed in the worship of Jehovah and the interpretation of those beliefs and how they should be followed and lived out.

Each of these groups found their own way of living under the Roman government. All were present in Jerusalem.

As almost always happens, the differences between the

groups became stronger and began to divide and separate these divergent schools of thought—each with its own leadership in place, and each becoming more extreme as time went on. Differences between these groups had grown vast, and each vied for supremacy in the leadership of the Hebrew Nation. During the hundred years BC (Before the birth of Christ), the Pharisees seemed to lead ahead of the second party, the Sadducees. The Pharisees were the more theologically allied, whereas the Sadducees tended more toward the legalistic and political direction, and often the chief priest of the nation came from the Sadducees.

During this time there was a member of the Pharisees who was of extremely high wisdom and had earned the respect of all who knew him—even the members of the Sadducees. He became known to all as a man who would speak from the history, the law, and the culture. His guidance to the leaders of the country had tremendous influence in the decisions made for the nation of Israel. This man was known as Hillel the Elder. Hillel the Elder became the teacher for most of those who were chosen to be in the organization of Pharisees, and from thence began the *School of Hillel*, in which all Pharisees and even many of the Sadducees wished to be a participant.

Hillel the Elder's date of birth is given as 100 BC, and he is known to have spent all of his life in study and sharing what he had learned. He lived to the age of one hundred and ten in a time when the normal life span was between forty to fifty years of age. The legacy of Hillel the Elder affected the thinking of the nation of Israel far into the future.

Into the family of Hillel the Elder came a grandson, actually a great grandson, who was given the name Gamaliel.

Hillel held this tiny grandson early, long, and often, and the little grandson became totally enthralled with his aging great-grandfather and the flowing long white beard which seemed to be longer than the boy himself. Each day Gam, as his great-grandfather nicknamed the boy, came running to be held in the gentle arms of this loving old man.

The word for grandfather, Sabba, was a simple word to say and easily learned. Gam and Sabba spent every possible minute of the day together. It was not surprising that the wisdom of the elder Hillel began flowing at a very early age to the younger Gamaliel, and as time would show, the mind of the young Gamaliel was open, available, and deep.

As Hillel began to realize the amazing ability of this boy-child, who was more and more left in his presence and care, he began to take careful and thoughtful consideration as to the content and quality of his teaching to this special child. Hillel believed that Jehovah, God, had given him Gamaliel to train with a special purpose in mind. Perhaps this was the time he could begin the teaching of a new concept he wanted to share.

This new concept had entered his mind during a time of meditation on God's promises to his people while traveling home from a visit to relatives in the hill country. There had been a death in the family and the passing of the family business to the eldest son was witnessed by the extended family members. On the way home, Hillel thought of how Jehovah had designed His plan for families, and then began to wonder if perhaps this same design would be used by Jehovah himself. Could and would Jehovah pass His work of guidance and forgiveness on to His own son? Jehovah had mentioned His son several times in the old writings, but Hillel had not as yet seen the plan of the Son of Jehovah and the part He would have in Jehovah's design for the world He had created.

This thought would not leave Hillel's mind, and he had many times since meditated on this very thing. Jehovah had also promised to send the *Messiah, (the anointed one)*, the one who was chosen and anointed to be the leader of God's chosen people. Was there a chance that Jehovah's own son would be that Prince of Peace? The more he thought about the connection of the two, the more sense it made to him. But how could he share this new thought of Jehovah and His son with the old school Sadducees and even the newer members of the Pharisees? Their first response would be to accuse him of blasphemy. New thinking was not easily accepted by either group. There was also the attitude of the scribes who felt they had total knowledge of all that had ever been written. This could be an extremely rocky road to travel. New ideas were always difficult to introduce and even more challenging to become accepted.

Just a few years before this time, Hillel saw the thoughts of the Pharisees moving away from the foundation which he felt God had established for the nation and His people. Hillel watched as the law as given to Moses was being adjusted, rearranged and sometimes thinned down in order to fit the political aspirations of the leaders who wished to conform to the rules of the Roman government. Hillel believed that the Mosaic Law was not to be compromised for any earthly government. He also believed it was possible to live under the Mosaic Law while under the confining laws of the Romans. He began the School of Hillel with the purpose in mind of training leaders in the original intent of the Law, and helping bring the belief in Jehovah back on track.

The most agonizing thing to Hillel was that while the primary laws were being observed by the leaders, the total concept of Jehovah as a loving, caring, and forgiving God was being pushed aside as not being important, especially now, under a powerful earthly Roman government. The promise of a Messiah had almost been forgotten in the constant desire to survive and succeed. The Messiah or "Anointed One" became a name for an earthly leader who would show them the way out from under the Romans and to lead the country of Israel back to greatness. This new concept of the Messiah had found its way into the Grand Sanhedrin and even the priesthood, but it diminished or even dismissed the love of Jehovah.

With the very small child nestled on his shoulder sleeping, Hillel began planning for the teaching he would begin to share with Gamaliel. He decided he would start immediately. Recognizing the age of this little one, he would change the words and the manner of instruction, but he would start right away. Sometimes adults were less than aware of the ability of a child's mind. A child could and would learn as much from the tone of voice and the attitude of love with which the words were spoken as they would from the words themselves.

Hillel knew that Jehovah had given him this opportunity to train a leader who could be part of the work to reshape and redirect the priests back to the original loving rules God had provided for them to follow. All of this was in Hillel's mind as he softly began humming and singing Psalms to the tiny child cuddled on his shoulder. Hillel started with Psalms of worship and praise and sang them lovingly for hours on end. The boy would look up into the face of the old man and see the love in his eyes, hear the gentle sound of his voice, and actually feel the vibrations from his chest as the hours went through the day. Hillel never tired of the effort it took to sing, and the child smiled, cuddled, and slept there in the arms of love by the name of Hillel.

The first formal word training that Hillel used was the Shema, "Hear Oh Israel: the Lord is our God, the Lord is One." This was taught to everyone from the earliest days of their lives. Understanding the importance of these words to the young members of the nation, Hillel repeated these phrases many times a day into the ears of the baby until Gamaliel could say them before he was able to put his own thoughts into any kind of order. Gamaliel's first words came almost at the same time as his first steps. His mother was only too happy to have the child spend so much time with the elder Hillel as it allowed her to keep ahead of the others of the family in the way she desired. The learning he received there from his great-grandfather was far more than she could provide while caring for the others of the family.

Hillel had many meetings with the other Pharisees, members of the Sadducees, and sometimes the whole of the Sanhedrin as they made most of the decisions pertaining to the national interest. Because of his position of high respect and the title of *Rabban*, (the senior Rabbi respected of all Rabbis), it was not denied the elder Pharisee, nor unusual for Hillel to even bring Gamaliel into the presence of the elders of Israel. The long walk and the high stone steps up to the Great Temple and into the room of meeting seemed not to even slow the elder Hillel down. In fact, having the child with him seemed to inspire him and give him more energy.

One lesson that kept itself foremost in the mind and heart of Hillel, was the love he believed Jehovah had for His people. He had gleaned from the old writings of the Law, the prophets, and even the books of writings, (or poetry), that Jehovah had an abiding and eternal love for his creation that even the failings and deliberate disobedience of Jehovah's chosen people could not change or remove. These thoughts were in the heart and mind of Hillel when he started the very highly esteemed School of Hillel ("Beit Hillel"), which became the main training school for the Pharisees. All who desired the title of "Pharisee" wanted to sit under the wisdom of Hillel and learn from this highly esteemed teacher. Even many of the Sadducees would come just to learn from the great mind of Hillel the Elder.

There was another school, "Beit Shammai", which differed from "Beit Hillel", and debated the teaching of the old law, but it is the School of Hillel which has had the longest lasting effect on Judaism. Because of his great wisdom and knowledge of the scriptures, Hillel was given the title of Rabban. This title was placed only upon the one who was respected as the wisest and most learned of all of the Pharisees.

THE FIRST PASSOVER FEAST FOR THE YOUNG GAMALIEL was when he was five. The capital city, Jerusalem, was packed with many times the number of people who actually called the city home. This feast was the most important feast of the nation of Israel as it remembered and celebrated the time that Jehovah had freed them from captivity in the land of Egypt. Jehovah had shown His immense and immeasurable power and love through a series of plagues upon the nation that held them captive. The Hebrew people had been spared from these plagues. The last of these ten plagues was the death of the firstborn of every household, even the animals. Jehovah had sent a messenger of death who passed over the land. Because of the promise marked by blood they were to put on their doorposts, the Hebrews escaped the death penalty. They were able to pack and leave for a journey to a new land that had been promised many years before to the founder, considered the father of the nation, by the name of Abraham. This *Feast of the Passover* was a yearly feast of celebration to remind the people of the ever sheltering love and care Jehovah had promised His people. This blood on the doorposts was given as an everlasting promise never to be forgotten, and was passed down through all generations.

Because this feast centered at the temple in Jerusalem, everyone who could would make the journey from wherever their home was, and the standard of the land was that hospitality was to be offered to all who came. Most of the buildings were built for sleeping on the roofs where there would be fresh air. So that is where guests, especially the men, slept when visiting. There was also enough air movement to make sleeping up higher in the open air cooler. That meant also that at this feast, the roofs were totally covered with sleeping mats.

The city was packed, and all were in a festive mood as this was also a time when families who had been separated by marriage or relocation were able to get together again. It was noisy, crowded, and going from one place to another was a slow, challenging process. This was also not a place for a five-year-old to hang on to the hand of a taller person. A boy this size rode on the shoulders of his father or grandfather for safety, and this is what Gamaliel did. With his eyes and his mind wide open to all that was going on around him, Gamaliel rode high on the shoulders of his father and took in everything he could mentally store. Not only were there the citizens of the Jewish nation, but there were merchants from seemingly every country of the known world. All of them were holding out their wares and calling out in a manner that was desired by its caller to be heard above everyone else. The sound was a competitive shouting match.

There were also animals being led up the narrow, crowded streets to the temple for sacrifice. As this was the primary feast of the year, the animals numbered in the thousands, and the sounds of confused sheep added to other animals and the vendors, each trying to be heard above all others, in order to sell their wares. This made the sound of the busy streets so loud it became difficult to even carry on a conversation. These celebrations became a regular part of the early life of the young Gamaliel.

# PART II

But the time had now come for Gamaliel to start his formal education under the local Rabbi. Almost all training outside of the home was done under the local or a favorite Rabbi. This was the beginning of learning in the company of other boys and the beginning of training for manhood.

Since almost all training was done by the local Rabbi, this position was very important and was chosen carefully by the parents. The choice of a teacher in the smaller villages was sometimes from among the most qualified of the men, but there were also times of difficulty where there would be a bit of travel to get to a quality teacher.

As the position of Hillel was so high, he was able to see that Gamaliel sat under the training of only the best of teachers. Hillel, as head of the School of Hillel, was teaching and training at an adult level and so left the normal schooling of the young to those who were skilled in that level of training. The subject in this, the first part of formal training for boys, was the Mikra. This was made up of the text, translation, reading and interpretation of the Holy writings of the Hebrews. There would be several years of this type of training lasting until the boys were about twelve. This was also intermixed with the family training in the trade of the fathers.

After school each day, Hillel took Gamaliel with him as he went to and from the temple. Hillel did this to see that the young Gamaliel was well acquainted with the Grand Sanhedrin and how it worked. Time on the street going to and from the temple gave Hillel a special touch to his personal time of teaching as it added the experiences of everyday life to the schooling under the local Rabbi. Hillel, as the Rabban, also saw to it that Gamaliel was exposed to only the most learned and wisest of the Rabbanim.

The training of this level always brought questions to the minds of the young students of this special age group. There were other students of high potential in this special training, and lifelong relationships and friendships were begun here. Questions and stories, called parables, were the norm for teaching and conversation. This form of schooling was designed to create in the minds of the students deep thinking and meditation.

Soon there came the time for more questions from the young Gamaliel to his great-grandfather. Hillel had always encouraged questions, and when the time grew near, he was prepared for these questions as they many times came out in a rush. One of the questions was:

"We worship Jehovah, but why can't we see Him? The other

people have many gods and place them on a shelf or above their doors. Why do they only worship gods they can see? Their gods have many shapes and sizes and they carry them around, even in their pockets. Are they really gods? Why are their gods carved and shaped by men, for they are not all the same? Some are shaped like animals and some like strange creatures. If Jehovah is above all and greater than all other gods, why are these other gods used and worshipped? Do the people who have these gods know who Jehovah is? Why doesn't Jehovah show Himself to us?"

Hillel held up his hand to stop the torrent of words coming at him like a strong wind. "Ask these things one at a time and let's see if we can find answers for as many as we can," Hillel answered as he and Gamaliel sat down on the steps leading up to the temple where they had been going. "Now," said Hillel. "What is your first question?"

Gamaliel thought for a moment. "Most of the other boys my age who do not worship Jehovah have an image of a god they can see. They have a carving or a figure in their house and a shelf that it sits upon, but we have nothing that tells us or shows us what Jehovah looks like. How do we know what Jehovah looks like? Sometimes the others ask me why I can't tell them who Jehovah is or what He looks like. I just don't know what to say when they ask."

Hillel sat for a few moments thinking, and then looked at the young Gamaliel.

"Long ago when man was created by Jehovah, he was given certain directions he was to follow. But man, thinking he knew as much as Jehovah, did not listen and chose to go his own way. This was the beginning of our sinful side. Jehovah removed his visible presence from man and also removed man from the beautiful garden He had created for man to care for. Seeing that man was determined to go his own way, Jehovah allowed man to try on his own to live the life that was designed for him.

"Man has continually failed trying to serve and reach Jehovah on his own. Man is now not allowed to live by a vision of Jehovah; but only by faith in believing that He is, is man able to return to the original relationship Jehovah has designed for us. God has sent us messages through prophets and priests to show us the pathway back to Him and warn us of the penalty for those who choose to continue in their own way, but man is stubborn and rebellious.

"Jehovah is the God of eternal and all-consuming love. He is the supreme God, and will not allow anyone to usurp His place in our lives and His love for us. The commandments Jehovah gave to our ancestor, Moses, are complete and we are to believe and follow what was written. There will come a time when Jehovah will send a very special messenger, one who is especially anointed, to lead all back to Him. All who will follow this "Anointed One" will be welcomed as children.

"This has been promised by Jehovah through the Prophets, and we have looked forward to that "Anointed One" for a long time. He is called "Messiah" and I believe He will come soon. It is my hope to be able to see Him in my lifetime. I believe He will show us the true way back to the relationship of love that Jehovah designed for us. I do not know exactly how He will do this, but we need to be ready to follow Him when He comes."

"How will we know who He is?" was Gamaliel's next question.

"Ahhh!" said Hillel. "I cannot tell you that. The prophet Isaiah wrote that there was no special look about Him that we would recognize Him instantly, but Jehovah would also send one before Him to announce His coming. I find in the old scriptures that he would send someone as a father would send his own son to complete the work He has begun. There are many other things said about Him, but some of the writings even I do not fully understand; so we continue to wait and seek to understand, but we will always keep looking for the answers."

It was at that point that Gamaliel interrupted. "Does Jehovah have a son?"

Hillel laughed. "He said He does and I believe Him. I do not as yet know Him. Jehovah has not shown him to us. But when He does, I hope to be able to meet Him face to face. As good and great as Jehovah is, I can only imagine what His son would be like. Now, back to your studies."

As Gamaliel left, Hillel chuckled. That was a new question. It wasn't very often that he would get a question he was not able to answer. Gamaliel was far ahead of other boys his age, but still had much to learn. Even one with Gamaliel's abilities and training from Hillel—the most learned teacher of the land—must wait for the proper age before society would accept him as one of the leaders of the people of Jehovah.

Hillel sat and pondered the training he had given the young Gamaliel. This had become a daily habit, going back over the years of teaching, looking for any flaws in the words and statements he had spoken. Had he gone too fast? Had he tried to give him too much for his age? Had he shared his opinion more than the truth? Had he given him the right guidelines for maturing in the law and the traditions handed down by the fathers? Would Gam, from the teachings he had been given, be able to keep himself on the right way? Above all, had he been able to instill the love of Jehovah, as well as the laws, in the proper balance? Would his great grandson be able to keep strong in the beliefs even when many of the Rabbis—even those of the Sanhedrin—were tipping the balance toward the social interpretation of the law and away from the infinite love of Jehovah?

Gamaliel could now read the old writings fluently, speak the common language, and was also learning to be proficient in Greek. Gamaliel was also daily with other young men of his age who were not as serious nor proficient in their growth, and he was helping them with their skills.

EARLY THE NEXT MORNING, Hillel began by sending his students to locate the oldest of the historical scrolls. The room where the sacred scrolls were kept was on the other side of the temple mount, so the students would be at least two hours before returning to the classroom where Hillel held his classes. As he waited for them to return, he began thinking about the conversation he had with Gamaliel the evening before. Hillel had studied much on the son of Jehovah and also on the one called "Messiah", who would be sent to lead Jehovah's people back to the relationship that Jehovah had designed for His people. It was during these times when the students of the school were gone from the classroom on assignment that Hillel loved to meditate.

He would use these quiet times to meditate on the questions that had been brought up during the day, put his lessons for classes the next day in order, and search the scriptures for new insights to bring up for discussion during the next day's class. Young men who were serious students were always ready to listen to something they had not heard before. Anything that Hillel brought up as new was instantly accepted by these who were becoming men and preparing themselves to make decisions for the nation of Israel.

Perhaps it was time to bring into the minds of three special students he had been watching, the ideas he had been stirred with that day coming back from the funeral in the hill country. Hillel set about laying out how he would present this new idea to the always eager students.

# PART III

In the home of Gamaliel at the evening meal, the father of Gamaliel was asking him about some of the things he had studied over the years of his schooling, especially his personal thoughts and beliefs of Jehovah. The occasion was the very special time of the choosing of Gamaliel to serve on the area Sanhedrin. This was a very prestigious position and only those of great wisdom and integrity were considered for this position. Gamaliel had been chosen at an age far younger than the normal required age because of his demonstrations of wisdom that had been observed by all those with whom he had come in contact. Gamaliel was at this early age held in high respect by all and was known also because of his relationship and training of his great-grandfather, Hillel the Elder. Because of the high honor this choosing brought to the family, the father of Gamaliel chose to invite Gamaliel to share thoughts about his learning with the family.

The answer came in the most pleasing way his father could ever have asked. "I find myself drawn more to those laws which can only come from a Jehovah who far more loves us than one who asks His servants to live on rules alone. There is promise in a loving Jehovah where there seems to be only punishment in living by a rigid set of rules. There is above all other things, the promise of forgiveness in love, whereas the rules speak more of retribution. It is the promise of loving forgiveness which I wish to understand more. There is a promise of our return to the sharing relationship of love between a father and his children which Jehovah designed for us. The promise of love and our return to the home, where Jehovah wants us to dwell with Him, is found throughout all the laws we have been given."

There was a long silence as father and son looked directly at each other. Then the father of Gamaliel spoke. "It is a matter well chosen. What you have decided gives me confidence in your maturity and your thinking. That of which you wish to learn and share is not spoken of as often as it should be. The nation and especially our leaders have drifted to focusing on certain laws which they think are easier to use in order to adjust their lives and the lives of our people to fit the Roman overseers. When you are ready, I offer myself as a ready listener to all that which you have learned. If you are willing, I offer myself to help you with your manner of presentation to the others which is also very important. Sometimes the manner in which you speak is as important as the words and the thoughts you are sharing. Your listeners will not be only your family members, but also higher ranking members of the Sanhedrin, itself. Your great-grandfather personally has encouraged several chosen members of the Grand Sanhedrin to hear you, for it seems he is extremely proud of your learning." (There were area Sanhedrins in order to guide sections of the country, but the Grand Sanhedrin was located in Jerusalem. The local units normally were made up of twenty-three members, while the Grand Sanhedrin was made up of seventy-one.)

"I expected Sabba to do that, father. I look forward to your advice and guidance on this, for it is also my desire to bring pride to my family. I thank you in advance for your very learned assistance. I wish, above all, to speak words in a manner that is pleasing to Jehovah."

Gamaliel started the next morning with preparations for the life he had chosen and the message he had chosen to share. Every day he read and spoke his words aloud—sometimes in his room, sometimes in front of his father, who guided him as to the proper way to speak, and use vocal inflections to create the effect of the words to the greatest understanding of Gamaliel's interpretation. Reading aloud was the choice way of meditating on the Word of Jehovah, and the father of Gamaliel was also a man known for great wisdom and public speaking.

At last the special day had come for Gamaliel to speak to the area Sanhedrin and Gamaliel woke, prepared himself in his best robe, and found himself nervous even though he had prepared long and hard. As the time came closer for him to present his reading from the old scriptures, his father came to him. "It is now time, my son, for you to be part of the leaders of this great nation Jehovah has given us. I have come to personally tie your Tefillin to your head and arm as a statement of how proud I am of you. Our family and friends await your words."

With his father's smile and a hug of love, Gamaliel moved to the place at the front of the gathering where all eyes turned to hear this new member of the adult world begin his public speaking. Because of the many hours of practice, the words came easily. To Gamaliel, it was suddenly over, with others gathering around him, complimenting him on a quality message and manner of presentation. He was now part of—and accepted into—the Sanhedrin, and would help to make decisions for the nation's people.

ON THE FIRST DAY OF THE NEXT WEEK, Hillel the Elder sat down with Gamaliel and said, "It is now time for you to begin to focus on the purpose Jehovah has designed for your life. I believe you are ready and able to handle the challenges I lay out for those who come to me for training to prepare for the life of a Pharisee serving on the Sanhedrin. This training is wide and thorough, but you and I have already been working in that way, for I have long thought that your deep mind and thoughtful ways would be a tremendous benefit to those who sit on the high council. There are also some thoughts I have that are not generally known and accepted, and in fact would be considered blasphemy if spoken in public. It is these thoughts I will entrust to your keeping as we study. There are things that Jehovah has given to me which I have shared with no one else, only your father. As we study and learn together, we will find the truth and the way to bring this new idea to the Sanhedrin, the nation, and later the world. Tomorrow, we will begin, you and I, and perhaps Jehovah will give us some companions to share this new thought. Be ready, for the amount of study can be overwhelming.

At the same time Gamaliel was growing and learning in Jerusalem, there were two others who were also being trained in a similar way, both of similar age and with the desire and guidance to build them into the leadership for the future. One of these was the grandson of a businessman who had spent most of his life helping to grow a business in trade from the caravans coming through the city of Jerusalem. He was located just outside of the city on the trade route where the business was lucrative because he was able to see many of the wares before they got to the larger markets. His skill of being able to purchase the best of the merchandise from the caravans brought him to the point where he became one of the wealthier citizens of the area known as Arimathea.

He also was very selective in finding merchants, in Jerusalem and other larger towns, who would be able to sell for a substantial profit. This man Joseph taught his son, Abraham, who being a devout man, had been chosen to serve on the local Sanhedrin. Abraham was a member of the party of Pharisees and had also studied with Hillel, the Elder. Abraham's dream was for his son Joseph, named after his grandfather, to serve on the Grand Sanhedrin in Jerusalem.

Because of the dream of his father, Joseph the son had been sent, at much expense, to sit under the best teachers of the Pharisees—even to the School of Hillel. Here he had shown his great ability for learning and understanding the Mosaic Law. Hillel the Elder had taken notice of this Joseph and also was watching and waiting for him to make an appearance in leadership as he grew older.

It was in this period of schooling that Joseph met two other young men of his own age. These two were named Gamaliel and Nicodemus. The three became close friends, a friendship that was to last a lifetime. The three studied together, and built their understanding of the Law that was to be taken with them into the positions of leadership. They also received much special attention and training time in and out of the classroom from Hillel the Elder.

Joseph had early learned the trade business. Through time, his family had built a substantial and far reaching system which extended even across the great sea to Gaul, Greece, Rome, and even further. It extended past the great sea around to and into a greater sea, to the land now known as the British Isles. This business was well known to the Roman rulers, and they were known to often purchase from and ship their goods by this business.

As was the practice of the Hebrews, the trade business was passed down from father to son, and the son was expected to continue, expand, and excel in the business of his father. The wisdom shown by Joseph in his trade, and the schooling under Hillel, became an open door to his appointment to the area Sanhedrin. Joseph was invited at a younger than normal age to take a place on the local decision-making body. Here, he also grew to a place of leadership, earning the respect of all who knew him. He was noted for his dedication to the Law of Moses, and his love for those he guided. Joseph was often asked to speak in front of the gathering at his Synagogue, where he was held in high respect by all who heard him. He was especially known as a man who lived what he taught and would help anyone who asked of him. Joseph became known also as a man of extremely high intellect and was early suggested as a candidate for the Grand Sanhedrin in Jerusalem.

Nicodemus was part of another family that lived in Judea, close to Jerusalem, which also was focused on preparing their young boy for a future of leadership. He was the middle child of seven and had a willing heart toward all. His older siblings were constantly asking him to do things with them or for them, and the younger ones wanted to do anything he was doing just to be with him. The family was very close to one another and remained so as the children grew. Nicodemus, as he grew up, became known as a person with a great loving heart, always ready to help and serve anyone in need. When his mother would lose track of him, he could always be found close by offering to help a neighbor with whatever they were doing.

Nicodemus was also a person of great curiosity, always asking questions and seeking understanding of everything he saw or heard around him. His parents, recognizing his desire for learning, sought for him a place of greater education where his wondering mind could be filled. It was during this search that they heard that the great Hillel the Elder would accept a very few students of younger than normal school age and had an opening at the very time his parents were visiting Jerusalem. Hurrying to gain an audience with the great Pharisee, they brought Nicodemus to Hillel the Elder for a meeting.

Hillel was the most respected elder of Israel who was also extremely gracious to the parents as they introduced their son. After meeting with Nicodemus, Hillel saw in this boy the qualities he was looking for in his special students. As Hillel the Elder taught many of the Pharisees in preparation for a position on the Sanhedrin, he searched for those younger students with the special qualities that would make them a good leader and policy maker for the nation.

The first and highest quality Hillel was looking for was the love of all people. This was to Hillel the quality that Jehovah had imprinted on all the laws and guidelines He had given His people through the centuries. Beside this was a desire to know and follow the Mosaic laws and guidelines the old prophets had laid down for the nation. These qualities he found in young Nicodemus, with the additional quality of the desire to learn. Nicodemus was invited to join the special group under Hillel the Elder and was there joined in a special relationship to Gamaliel and Joseph.

These three became fast friends and gave tremendous joy to Hillel because of their open and willing minds. Hillel took the three boys under his personal care and guidance as he would his own sons. He believed that Jehovah also had a family as indicated by his speaking of His Son and therefore attempted to emulate the kind of care that he thought Jehovah would want for His own Son.

The next day they began the schooling, studying the differences of thoughts that had prevailed and developed over the years since the founding of the nation of Israel. These different schools of thought were all begun by earnest, believing people, each school believing they alone had the only correct way to interpret and guide the nation under the Mosaic laws.

Their studies began with the focus on the law as written by Jehovah through Moses. Then there were the prophets with the interpretations and perceptions of the law and special messages to the people of Jehovah. Added to this and integrated into the mix were the writings, the stories, and books of poetry. All studies were adorned with the singing of Psalms and hours of prayers and worship to Jehovah. When they reached a high level of this training, they began to learn the political history of each tribe and time period of every government which had ruled over the country. After these things, they studied the different parties which they were being trained to participate in and lead.

The first party to be formed was the Sadducees who, over the years, became focused on the letter of the law as handed down by Moses. This gave rise to a form of legalistic belief where ritual moved to the forefront and the true meaning of worship which was honor to Jehovah, was slowly pushed aside and replaced by the focus on rules and regulations. This hid the real understanding of Jehovah, the meaning of the worship, and the sacrifices held in the temple. This then changed into a man-designed form of belief where rules were adjusted for the benefit of those who were leading, and making the relationship to Jehovah adjust to whatever government was in charge. Because the rules were easy to see, faith was pushed to the wayside. The afterlife was lessened in belief, and the "Anointed One", later called "Messiah", was altered to be only an earthly leader who would drive out the prevailing government and bring Israel back to earthly glory.

The Pharisees were started much later than the Sadducees and with not only the intention of restoring the relationship with Jehovah, but also the quality and the purpose of the temple worship and sacrifices. They also were founded on the law as handed down by Moses, but felt that the spoken law was important alongside the written word. There were also many interpretations of the laws added, and these over time became to the Pharisees almost as important as the laws themselves.

The group known as scribes were those who spent their life

copying the old scriptures, and because of the time they spent studying, felt they were the ones who knew the words best. Their opinions were heard, especially when questions arose, but they really had very little authority or impact on the decisions made by the high council, the "Grand Sanhedrin".

There was a smaller group that was mostly of the Pharisees but felt they were unable to maintain the pureness of their lives and the law in the middle of the society in which they lived. They therefore separated themselves from the others in areas of the city of Jerusalem and some even went out into the Judean wilderness and built enclaves in which to live by their strict rules. They were known as the Essenes and strove to live at a level above others of their faith.

A small group called Zealots focused on the political hatred of the ruling Romans. This group would stoop to any means available, even assassination, to affect the governing of the nation, moving it to the way they thought was right. These men were well skilled in locating a target, stabbing the person in the back, and yelling for help for the victim while escaping in the gathering crowd.

With this introduction to the governing of Israel, Gamaliel and his two friends began the next few years of their lives learning more about the people and the way they thought. They would go out among the crowds on many days, spend as much time in the temple as possible with those who came there, and go and visit people in different areas and occupations. Their goal was to learn as much as possible about the people of Jehovah and how they lived. The primary action after spending time out among the people, was spending the evening discussing the things they had heard and learned and how this knowledge could and should be used in the capacity of the nation's leadership. The goal of this learning was to become a Godly image and also to become an intelligent and learned leader. They early became known as teachers who were respected for their deep thought and commitment to Jehovah's ways and the Law of Moses. It was because of their love of the law and at the same time love of the people around them that they drew others to themselves.

Hillel had consistently and carefully instilled in these three men the concepts that he believed had been handed down by Ezra, the priest who had been allowed to return to Jerusalem from Babylon to rebuild the temple and beliefs of the Hebrew people. These concepts were for them to be peaceful men and lovers of all men. They were also to be diligent students but always ready to teach others with persuasiveness of the truth. In all learning, they were to be thorough, accurate in their speaking about the law, their lives showing forth cheerfulness, demonstrating a total trust in God.

Gamaliel, Joseph, and Nicodemus early earned the title of "teacher". They became addressed as "Rabbi", and naturally were appointed to positions of leadership. They were also appointed each to their local Sanhedrin at similar times in their prospective areas. Being from different areas, their meetings together as friends became less frequent, but the friendship did not waver, and every time they were able to get together was looked upon with great anticipation. It would only stand to reason that they would also be in time appointed to the Grand Sanhedrin in Jerusalem.

It was there that Gamaliel again began meeting often with Hillel, Joseph, and Nicodemus, all of whom were of like thought in learning and focus on the Mosaic Law. It was this trio of quality Pharisees that Hillel the Elder again brought together to share his passion about the Messiah, the Son of Jehovah, and the combining of the two thoughts into one person of promise of what they had come to believe—that the Messiah would be the actual son of Jehovah.

The more they studied, the more they realized they were correct in their beliefs about this matter. The first concept of a ruler beyond and above any other ruler in the future began to take fertile seed in the writings of Isaiah, and from that seed the word "Messiah", or "Anointed One" grew until it became the common word of usage for the one who would come and remove Israel from under all earthly governments and establish it as a kingdom over all kingdoms on earth.

At this time, the Roman government ruled most of the known world, and the leaders of the Sanhedrin were careful not to upset the balance that had allowed them to have some power over their small country. Therefore, it was not possible for Gamaliel, Joseph, and Nicodemus to be extremely open in their opinions to the total group of the Sanhedrin as there was always someone who would be ready to charge them with wrong beliefs, even blasphemy. This was the most serious charge to be laid upon anyone and almost always carried the punishment of death by stoning. Even with the prevailing Romans having the last word of the sentence of death, it was often possible for the Roman leadership to turn their backs when the Jewish people carried out this death sentence on one of their own. As long as it did not affect Roman law, the Roman soldiers did not interfere. For this reason, the trio who had accepted this new thought did not widely announce their beliefs but kept them quiet, and secretly sought out others, one at a time, who they believed were open to this new way of thinking.

The concept of the future king of all was brought forth by the prophet Isaiah, and from this time the word "Messiah" began to take root among the common people. The term came to mean the future king of Israel who would be anointed above all others, past, present, and future. The leaders of the nation, being under control of an earthly government, took it to mean the deliverance from whoever was in control of the country at that particular time. Therefore, at this time, the Messiah would be the deliverer from the Roman government. The real meaning was faded or lost in the daily thoughts as the people focused on the needs of their daily lives.

# PART IV

Over time there were some small happenings in the temple of Jerusalem that were noted but quickly forgotten by the majority of the priests and other officials of the temple. Because of the rotation of the priests across the country to serve in the temple in Jerusalem, as it was the seat of Jewish worship, all happenings were carefully screened by the priests and rabbis to make sure everything was done in the proper order within the rules set down for temple worship and visitation. But within these rules and the great walls of the temple in Jerusalem there were things that were not recorded and therefore easily forgotten.

There were two elder worshipers who stayed at the temple praising God and worshiping constantly. These two were known to all who came and were looked upon with favor by all who came to the temple. These two, after many years, suddenly spoke out about one child who had been brought for his dedication. This was unusual, as these—Simeon and Anna

—were noted for their quietness and dedication to God; and shortly after the happening of them speaking, were gone. They had actually spoken over the same child, but this was not given any special significance by the priests serving their rotation duties in the temple, as people, especially people this old, died every day. So hereupon, the priests were not long in forgetting the words that had been spoken or the people who had spoken them. The words spoken by these two older people were of the future and added to the storehouse in the mind of Hillel, for they were of immense importance.

These two people were well known to Hillel the Elder who had conversed with them frequently and had listened carefully. All the things they had been saying were kept in the heart of Hillel. So it was that Hillel was quickly aware of the child over which these two had prophesied. The words they had spoken had never moved far away from the thoughts of Hillel, and he found himself returning to those words again and again. He especially remembered Anna speaking in a strong voice which had not been the normal manner of her prayers.

There was also at a later time, a young visitor to the temple who tarried after his parents had left, staying in the presence of the priests and rabbis who were serving their rotation in the temple, questioning them and listening to them with great understanding. Although those who were in those times of service were greatly astonished at his comprehension, this too passed quickly as nothing more than a passing thought. It seems that he was from Galilee, and no one from that area was thought to have the theological understanding of the Mosaic Law.

As the duty of the priests was of regular rotation, those who were there went back to their homes and the moment was again soon forgotten. He was also from a family of the common people and therefore carried a reputation of no significance. Hillel the Elder was in the temple that day and although not in the discussion that took place between the boy and the priests, listened to most of what was said from both the priests and the boy. Hillel's heart was filled with a joy he did not understand at the time, but he also could not lose the feeling that kept coming back each time he brought that day to remembrance. Neither could he forget the words the boy spoke to his mother when she scolded him lightly. "Didn't you know I would be about my father's business?" It was a very strange answer, indeed.

Hillel the Elder had collected everything that his great mind would hold and put every fact together as you would a great puzzle, and from this he called the three friends together and began a special discussion which he urged them to keep to themselves.

He began, "Many years ago, I shared with you my thoughts about Jehovah and the "Anointed One" who is promised to be sent by Jehovah to the nation. I believe the time may be upon us for that to happen. A couple brought a baby to the temple for the normal dedication of the firstborn son, but this one was different, as there were two elder people well known by all in the temple who spoke over and about this particular child. There was also more recently the occasion that a young boy came into the temple at the end of the Passover and when his parents had left for the journey home, he stayed in the temple speaking with the priests about the Law of Moses and the interpretation of the law as it was applied to the people of Jehovah. His understanding of the law was amazing and absolutely correct. Even the most learned of the priests were speechless and said they had never encountered a youth so filled with understanding. I believe we are closer to the promise of Jehovah than ever before."

It was just a few years later that Hillel the Elder died at the age of 110 years. This was an extremely long life, as the average lifespan was under fifty years at that time. He was mourned by all who knew him or studied under his teaching. He left a legacy of training that would last for many centuries.

# PART V

Gamaliel, Joseph, and Nicodemus continued as friends, and although they were regularly meeting and concerned with the current events over which they helped sit in judgement and advised the leaders and priests, they never forgot the one idea that had been brought to their minds and hearts by Hillel the Elder about the Messiah being the Son of Jehovah.

This was often brought up as they were always looking in the old writings handed down to them and at the same time looking forward to the time when Jehovah would send His Messiah, the "Anointed One," to the people of Israel. Hillel had also left them with the belief that it was close to the time for the Messiah of Jehovah to come and lead Israel back to the original love relationship Jehovah had designed for His creation.

The three friends not only spent much time together, much of the time was spent in study and prayer, and the three friends developed a reputation for the highest level of knowledge, integrity, and wisdom. Their ability to bring to the Grand Sanhedrin the best interpretation and applications of the words of those who had passed long before aided greatly in quality decisions being made in the great meeting room.

# PART VI

Then, after what seemed like many years, a new story began to come to the ears of the Grand Sanhedrin about a wild man teaching in the Judean wilderness. This new wilderness speaker, who was dressed in camel's hair, shouted the message, "Repent, for the Kingdom of the Lord is at hand!"

When the three met together the first time after this news had come to their hearing, the discussion was not about the dress of this new person, but about the message he was proclaiming. The words he was speaking were from Isaiah, the ancient Prophet, and landed on the ears of these three Pharisees with a special significance.

As the three began discussing this new messenger, the stories and teachings of Hillel the Elder came back with a new fervor and they began to gather everything they had been taught over the years of study and apprenticeship—especially the words of Isaiah. It was at this point that they sent several of their students to the area where this wild man, John by name, was speaking in the Jordan Valley. When the students returned, the questions raised were of a slightly different concept. All those in the past who had come with the claim of Messiahship were easily disputed, and their claims found to have no merit. Most just faded out after a very short time and a small following. Some were actually executed as enemies of the Roman State. However, this time when the students returned, the reports were of a concept and depth different from others that had previously come to their ears. All three Pharisees felt there was something different about this man and his message. They were excited as they made plans to visit personally, to hear this wilderness speaker. After all, they had been trained by Hillel, who had proclaimed that to visit the people where they lived was needed in order to better understand the call to leadership.

They set out to go and find out for themselves what this was all about. After two days' travel, they arrived at the place by the Jordan River where John—who was now called "The Baptizer"—was said to be speaking and baptizing. John was baptizing out in the wilds of Judea and not in the normal ceremonial pools where cleansing for worship was most often done.

Baptism was used by many beliefs of that day as a means of making a statement of change from one belief to another. (This action was also to cleanse away any impureness of the old beliefs and prepare and purify for the new belief.)

They remained standing at a distance where they could see but not get involved with the crowd. From their place on the bank of the river they could hear the words of the Baptizer, "I am the voice of one crying in the wilderness, make straight the way of the Lord," as the prophet Isaiah said.

There were other Pharisees at the river that day asking John why he was baptizing, for baptizing was used by the Hebrews for ritual cleansing, before worship, and before even entering the temple. They also asked him if he was the Christ (Anointed One).

John's answer came back not as expected when he said, "I baptize you with water, but one is coming who is mightier than I, and I am not fit to untie the thong of His sandals. He will baptize you with the Holy Spirit and with fire. His winnowing fork is in His hand to thoroughly clear His threshing floor, and to gather the wheat into His barn; but He will burn up the chaff with unquenchable fire."

John said other things, but the three friends were looking around at the people gathered by the Jordan. They did not see anyone who stood out from the crowd. They turned finally and started back to Jerusalem, their minds spinning with what they had seen and heard, finding new questions to ask one another. They were followed by their group of students who had followed them that day. The students were also murmuring among themselves about the day's happenings.

The next day, after dismissing their students early, they went to the home of Gamaliel and talked long into the evening, discussing old writings and teachings. They did find in the old words where it said that there would be nothing special in the appearance of the Messiah to announce who He was. At the end of the evening, it was decided to have the students return again to watch and bring back reports each day for a period of time. Gamaliel and his friends spent the day in study, meditation, and prayer for the coming of the Messiah.

The next day they called the young men who were studying under them to send them back to the Jordan to listen and observe John "The Baptizer", in order to keep up with events connected with this particular teacher and also to watch for anything special or out of the ordinary. There had been many men over the past two hundred years who had claimed to have a special message from Jehovah, and these students were familiar with the names of most of those past attempts to start a "Jehovah" movement. Some even claimed to be the Messiah. The directions given to the students were to watch for something special, but also to be especially watchful for any errors in John's teaching that might go against the Mosaic Law.

Matthew was the one who was chosen by the other group members to give the report when the students came again to meet at the home of Gamaliel in the evening. The report was not as anticipated. This is what Matthew, with many additions and interruptions from the others, shared with the trio of Pharisees.

"We found John at his regular place in the Jordan river where people could enter the Jordan with gentle steps in order to be baptized. All was normal except for one man who came and presented himself to John for baptism. John stopped him with these words, 'I have need to be baptized by you.' To which came the return, 'Permit it at this time, for in this way it is fitting for us to fulfill all righteousness.'

"When this man, who was then baptized by John, walked out of the water, there was a loud sound, like thunder and we heard a voice speaking with the words. 'This is my beloved Son in whom I am well pleased.' We also saw a beautiful dove come and alight upon Him. This man then turned and left toward the Judean wilderness and was seen no more by us.

"We did not know this man, but John seemed to be personally familiar with him and knew who he was. This was at the end of the day, and as the crowd had begun dissipating, John also left to the cave where he lodged between appearances at the Jordan. This was the only happening that we observed that was anywise different than the daily preaching and baptizing."

"And you were not able to learn his name?" asked Nicodemus.

"Nor from where he came?" added Joseph.

"Did you see who was speaking?" This from Gamaliel.

"We do not know who was speaking; but we all saw a beautiful dove come and light on him. We also do not know whether he will return or not," added another, "but we are willing to go and talk to others tomorrow to see if more can be learned."

The three Pharisees instantly agreed to this suggestion, and the students, ever ready for a new adventure, hurried to their own places of residence to ponder the day's events and make ready for the next day's visit to the Jordan preacher, John the Baptizer. The three who were chosen to seek further as to the identity of the man who they had seen baptized in the Jordan River were Matthew, Hilkiah, and Shaphan. These were the best of the students of the school under the teaching of Gamaliel and had earned a reputation for being of high integrity. Later they would also become appointed to the Grand Sanhedrin.

In a very short time the preaching of John by the Jordan River had become a focus of the Grand Sanhedrin, and there were Pharisees going regularly in turns to watch and report on this outspoken man of the wilderness. Actually, the number of Pharisees who were going to the river was growing, and as they had stood afar off and not participated in the crowd who pushed to enter the water under the hand of John, they drew his attention. John's remark to the Pharisees was not one that was pleasant, as he addressed them as a "brood of vipers." This insult was taken to heart, and the Pharisees were very careful not to get any closer to him but sent their students to bring them daily reports. They chose to consider him as one of the outsiders who had nothing of importance to say even though their anger toward him continued to grow.

This attitude of anger was not one taken by Gamaliel, Joseph, and Nicodemus as they followed the preaching of John through their students and servants. They were comparing his words closely with the Mosaic, prophetic, and historic writings they had been studying all their lives. Everything they had read and were now hearing was fitting together.

Suddenly, in an action that was all too usual under the Roman rule, John "The Baptizer" was beheaded. There were stories about why, but it seemed that John had spoken about certain sins of the king and had angered the king's wife who had staged a request for John's head to be taken off.

It was not long before they began hearing about unusual events associated with another teacher by the name of Jesus of Nazareth from the area of Galilee, the northern part of Israel. Most of what they were hearing came from visitors who had come to Jerusalem to see families, but soon the name of Jesus had found its way into more and more of the homes and normal street conversations. Everywhere they went in the city, they could hear people asking, "who was this Jesus?" People were even asking Gamaliel about Him, but Gamaliel had no answer he wished to give.

Gamaliel called his two friends Joseph and Nicodemus to meet and said, "Sabba always told me that if I wanted to know something, I should be part of it myself. I will take four students and travel to Nazareth to learn of this Jesus. I have heard that his mother was named Mary. This will be a trip where I can teach and instruct the students about the land and its people while we travel. We will leave early the first morning after the Sabbath, and be gone several weeks."

Gamaliel chose four of his best students, and the five men left as planned. As they traveled, Gamaliel began discussions with the students over the things they had been taught, starting with times of quizzing to bring up different parts of their education. As the road, or path, was quite rocky and uneven, there were times of stopping and resting. The students were to always be observant of the people they met and greeted and to store in their hearts and minds everything they could remember about those with whom they talked.

It was a long and hot trip and the way north they took was not straight as they had to circle around the area of Samaria. This was because of the high position of Gamaliel on the Sanhedrin. This detour made the trip two days longer, but because Gamaliel was a senior member of the ruling body and very highly respected, it was necessary that he also follow the rules the Sanhedrin had established for maintaining cleanliness required of a member of that body. Even passing through a corner of Samaria was considered to make one unclean.

Samaria was the part of the country that lay between Judea in the south and Galilee in the north. The people who lived there were considered half breeds and not true Jews. The stopping times were great for teaching and Gamaliel used them effectively, adding to the stores of knowledge already in the younger men's minds, expanding on what they asked, and answering other questions as they arose.

At last the town of Nazareth came in sight and all gave a sigh as they had come to the end of their journey. Gamaliel left the others setting up the camp and he went in search of the inn, which in those days was the place to obtain information. The innkeeper instantly recognized the robes worn by a member of the Grand Sanhedrin and his mind became filled with questions as he greeted and welcomed one of such high esteem to his inn. The innkeeper was also given to conversation, and as Gamaliel sat quietly and plied the innkeeper with leading questions, he learned all he needed to know about the family of Jesus.

When returning to Nazareth after traveling for long periods of time, Jesus would stay at the home of James the carpenter, his younger brother, where his Mother, Mary, also lived. After hearing much that he wanted to know, Gamaliel asked for directions to where the family was living. The innkeeper told Gamaliel where the house of James was located, and then added that James was a carpenter of high quality.

Gamaliel walked thoughtfully following the directions of the innkeeper to the front of the house which had a medium-sized carpenter's shop built next to it. He announced himself in a gentle manner, saying that he was looking for the family of Jesus. A woman came to the front, joined by her husband, and then a second woman who was some years older showed behind the first. The man of the house who introduced himself as James, a brother to Jesus, asked if there had been trouble, as it was most unusual to have a visitor of this high level of Jewish government to come to this small town, and especially to this house. The other children became respectfully quiet as Gamaliel was invited in and they realized the importance of this visitor. As everyone moved to their places on the cushions, all eyes turned to this special visitor.

To satisfy their unspoken curiosity, Gamaliel quickly assured them he was here not for a legal visit, but for a far more gentle conversation—one seeking information with which to satisfy his personal questions. At this, the women of the house went to bring food for the guest. James introduced them as Mary, his wife, and the older woman as Mary, the mother of Jesus. He motioned Gamaliel to sit down, as they of this house wished also to now satisfy their own curiosity which had been greatly aroused.

When they were gathered around the low table, and proper greetings had been said, Gamaliel looked at Mary and began. "We have been hearing about many happenings around the country from people of all tribes and areas concerning your son, Jesus. Many of these are about healings, signs, and other things being described as miracles. Although we have heard similar things before about other small groups with a leader, we now find that the stories about Jesus have seemed to come closer and closer to the stories and to the prophesies in the old writings of our people. I have spent my life studying the old laws, writings, and prophesies. I ask you now if there is anything you can tell me to explain why this man, Jesus, your son, should stand apart and be able to show forth such image and power. Was there anything different about his birth that would give evidence to what I am seeking? I ask not to accuse, but for my own knowledge and learning."

Mary looked at her son James and his wife who had now joined them on the cushions, and at their nod of approval, Mary began her story. "Even here in Nazareth have we heard the name of Gamaliel and his concern and love for the people of our country. I do not tell this story often but have kept it deep in my heart, for I know the facts are true and Jehovah has given Jesus to us as a nation and for all people. Perhaps it is time for others to hear."

Mary took a breath and then began.

"Many years ago I was asleep on my mat when I was awakened in the middle of the night by a bright light and a heavenly being who told me he was an angel. This angel told me to not be afraid for I had found favor with Jehovah. I would bear a son who was to be named Jesus. He would be great and be given the throne of his father, David, and would reign over the house of Jacob forever. I asked the angel how could this happen as I was unmarried and had not known a man. He answered me and said that the Holy Spirit would come over me and the child to be born would be called the Son of God. My mother sent me to visit a cousin named Elizabeth who we had heard was also pregnant even though past the age of bearing children. When I approached her house and she greeted me, the babe in her womb leaped for joy. Thus was I confirmed. When I returned home, my father went to tell my husband-to-be, who was called Joseph, what had happened, for we were not as yet married. Joseph asked for time to think and pray about this situation which had been pressed upon us. But in the middle of the night Joseph was told by an angel in a dream to come and take me to his home as his wife, for the baby was of the Holy Spirit. He rose and came immediately in the night to my father and brought me to his house, but did not know me as his wife until this Holy Child was born.

"Then we, like many others were ordered by the Roman government to go to the city of our fathers for the census. We traveled to Bethlehem, for both Joseph and I are of the house and lineage of David. While in Bethlehem, the baby, Jesus, was born. That very night shepherds came from the nearby fields to the stable where we were staying, telling us they had been visited by countless numbers of angels, filling the skies with much singing and telling them of the baby lying in the manger.

"As the census was going to take some time, my husband Joseph, a carpenter by trade, had brought tools and found work to sustain our family.

"Almost two years later, we were suddenly visited by an extremely large caravan escorting fourteen high dignitaries who came to visit this child, Jesus. They told us they were from a country far east of where we were and were guided by a star that had appeared in the night sky. The time the star first appeared was the same time as the birth of Jesus. After presenting costly gifts for the child, they left suddenly in the night, and in that same night, Joseph was awakened again by an angel who told us to flee to Egypt, for Herod, the king, would seek this child to take his life. We arose from our bed and found a small caravan trader who accepted us as members of his group. We went to Egypt and were there when we heard of the death of Herod. We then returned to Nazareth where we have stayed. Joseph trained our sons as carpenters but has been dead now several years. After Jesus left, my son James, who is also a carpenter by trade, has cared for me in his home where we are today.

"When the angel first came to me, he also gave me titles that would be given to this child that I have kept to myself. Perhaps they are for your ears as I have kept them deep in my heart and have yet to share these with any other. The angel said He would be called the "Son of Jehovah". He would sit on the throne of David, and would reign over the house of Jacob forever."

Gamaliel sat quietly for a few minutes and then he exclaimed, "The prophet said, 'He will be called Immanuel, God is with us.' This Jesus, your son, is the promise of Jehovah. Jesus is His own Son! Jesus is the Messiah! The Anointed One! The future King Jehovah chose to rule over Israel and the whole world forever!" Gamaliel bowed his face to the floor and gave praise to Jehovah. The family joined in as from their hearts they realized they had been chosen by Jehovah to share in this time of promise to the whole world.

After a time of praise and blessings, Gamaliel took his leave of the household and gathering his students, began the trip back to Jerusalem, his mind spinning with the attempt to put everything together. The things the angel had told the mother of Jesus, combined with the teaching his great-grandfather, Hillel the Elder, had given him over many years, made the news he was returning with all more exciting every minute. He could not wait to share with his friends Joseph and Nicodemus the many thoughts this visit to Nazareth had confirmed. His steps were light and his heart gave him new energy on the way back to Jerusalem.

The long trek from Nazareth south to Jerusalem over the stony, winding path that was called a road seemed to take longer than it did on the way north. Gamaliel was in a hurry to return to Jerusalem and decided he would go straight through Samaria.

As they traveled, Gamaliel talked with the students about the things he had assigned to them, but he also shared the good news that this trip had given to them. The students were nervous about the route but trusted their teacher and said little about the way they were taking. They had been told to learn as much as possible from people living in this area of the nation, but the news of the visit to the home of James became the most important topic.

Now the discussion moved to how they thought the Grand Sanhedrin would receive this news. Anyone thought worthy of leadership and also news of any special happenings that would be good to be shared with the leaders in Jerusalem was discussed, but nothing was as exciting as the things that had been confirmed to them by this visit to the home of James where the mother of Jesus was now living.

The nation of Israel had been waiting for this news for many years, and this small group was now on the way to Jerusalem to share what they had learned. How the leaders in Jerusalem would accept the revelation that Jesus was the long awaited Messiah was the question. The other travelers with Gamaliel were students and servants, and though it was difficult, Gamaliel did not share everything he had learned with them as he wanted to share with Joseph and Nicodemus first. He knew the students would not be able to keep from telling their friends and he did not want the wrong message to go forth until it was prepared properly.

The other two of the trio of Pharisees had been waiting anxiously for the return of Gamaliel as there were other stories about this Jesus being spread about by travelers, adding to the questions they already had. The stories of Jesus had spread all over the city of Jerusalem and even out to the surrounding towns, more since Gamaliel had left on his journey to Nazareth. Going immediately to the room Gamaliel had set aside for their meeting, they sat down and waited attentively for the words of Gamaliel.

"Neighbors," he began. "My trip was indeed not in vain, for I was welcomed into the house of James and was able to meet with the mother of Jesus and this is the story she shared with me of his birth. She was espoused to a young man named Joseph and planning for the marriage when one night, while she was lying on her mat in the space given to her for sleeping, she was awakened from sleep by a bright light and arose to the appearance of an angel. The angel told her his name was Gabriel and he stood in the presence of Jehovah. He told her to not be afraid for she had found favor with God and would become pregnant and would bear a son who was to be named Jesus and would be given the throne of David. He would reign over the House of Jacob forever. His kingdom would have no end."

"She said, 'I asked the angel how this was to happen as I had never known a man and am a virgin. The angel told me the Holy Spirit would come over me and the child would be called the Son of God. The angel also told me that my aging cousin, Elizabeth, was at that time also expecting a child, even in her old age, for nothing is impossible with God.' She said, 'I told the angel I would do as God asked. The angel left. In the morning I told my mother about the visit of the angel and the message I was given and that I had agreed to do as the angel asked. My mother sent me to visit Elizabeth, whose husband was a priest, and when Elizabeth greeted me, the baby in her womb seemed to dance in joy for she was in her sixth month. When Elizabeth felt the baby dancing, she greeted me by calling me the mother of her Lord. I stayed for a period of time, leaving when Elizabeth's time for her baby was near, and returned home to await my time. My father had to go to my betrothed and beg forgiveness for I, being with child was considered to have been unfaithful. That very night, an angel appeared to Joseph, my betrothed, in a dream and told him to take me home as his wife, as the child within me was of the Holy Spirit. The angel told Joseph she would have a son and you will call Him Jesus, for He will save his people from their sins.

'Joseph rose from his bed, came to my father and took me home as his wife even though we were not married. Joseph did not know me until after this child, Jesus, was born. We were waiting for the birth as God directed when the census came, and as we were both from the lineage of David, we left to go to Bethlehem, the city of David, where Jesus was born. We were staying in a small corner of the stable of the inn, as the town of Bethlehem was so crowded with the traveling of people for the census, this was the only place we could find. There, in the stable, Jesus was born. We were visited that same night by shepherds from the hills outside of the village who told us they had been told by a huge host of angels where to visit the child and that they would find their savior there in the stable. We made our lodging there in Bethlehem in a home after the birth in a house owned by the tax collector and Joseph worked at his profession, carpentry, as the census was expected to take several years. It was almost two years later that we were visited by some high officials from a country a great distance to the east and a huge caravan bringing us wonderful gifts for the child, Jesus. After they left their gifts, they suddenly left in the night. But, during that same night, Joseph, my husband was again aroused from sleep by an angel who told him to rise and take the child and myself to Egypt for safety, for Herod the king would seek the child to kill Him. We left that very night, traveling with a trader to Egypt. We stayed in Egypt until we heard that Herod had died and then returned to Israel, coming to Nazareth as we learned Herod's son was then in power. Here, in Nazareth, you see us still. The words I have given you today are true. I have kept these words and happenings in my heart. I know not how God will bring all His words to pass, but I trust Him to keep His promises.'"

Gamaliel stopped after his story, waiting for a period of time for the others to think about and to combine and adjust their teaching from Hillel the Elder with what they had just learned. It was more than they had hoped for. Gamaliel looked them in the eye and said, "I believe God has sent His own son to be the promised Messiah that Israel has been waiting for. This Jesus is the Messiah! Jesus is the Son of God!"

The three Pharisees bowed with their faces to the floor as they praised Jehovah for the fulfillment of the promise made long ago about the "Anointed One" coming to the people of Jehovah.

Then there was a long period of total quiet as the realization of their dreams sank into the hearts and minds of the three longtime friends. Then, another long space as the story of the birth of Jesus found its place in their thinking of this new confirmation of their study, and then to their positions on the Grand Sanhedrin, the highest decision-making group of the Jewish nation even while under the Roman occupation.

All three had been chosen for their position because of their known wisdom, and if they came out with this new idea that this Jesus of Nazareth was actually God's own Son, they could and would be charged with blasphemy and most likely publicly stoned.

There were already statements being made in the great meeting hall about how to control this new teacher, Jesus, and stop Him from continuing his teaching. They needed to proceed very carefully and share their thoughts on an extremely careful basis. There were even some of the more powerful members of the Grand Sanhedrin stating that they thought that the miracles being attributed to this Jesus were false signs and already drawing away from the focus they desired for their positions on the high council of the Grand Sanhedrin. There were actually some who were thinking that Jesus had been sent by the evil one to mislead the people of the Hebrew nation away from Jehovah. The last meeting had become a shouting match as everyone had a different story or report.

Then, the unthinkable happened. This Jesus had walked into the temple courtyard with a small whip, loosed all the animals being held for sale there, and threw the coins of the money changers all over the floor. This buying and selling was a huge abuse of the temple area, but no one was willing to use their authority to go against the High Priest. The High Priest had not only encouraged the market, but had also made a way to achieve great profit for his personal coffers. And so it continued. Animals which were brought in for sacrifice were routinely found to be unclean for some small reason, and then taken to an area, (often in the fields near Bethlehem), where they were held until they were rated as clean, and then sold in that same temple market at a later time for profit to someone else. Since almost all people brought an offering in the form of an animal, this was a huge form of wrongful profit-taking. Jesus publicly challenged this practice and acted against it, offending greatly those who were becoming wealthy by cheating others.

The conversation among the three Pharisees was much agitated when this was happening, for they were also aware of the wrong in the temple and although they had spoken quietly against it, had not been able to stop it as they were terrifically outnumbered and had found no one who would stand with them to protest. Among themselves, they were pleased at what had taken place when Jesus acted in this manner, but did not openly praise the action. The whole buying and selling in the temple square had become known as "Annas' Bazaar", (Annas being the high priest), and the actions of this new teacher, Jesus, were interpreted as a challenge to those in the higher levels of the Sanhedrin and their personal leadership. By doing what he did, He was also exposing the weaknesses and wickedness in their teachings and their leadership.

The idea came into being to trap Him with his own words. The more powerful Pharisees began going out in small groups, conniving together how to ask questions in a way so as to cause him to give an answer which could be interpreted for their personal benefit. But, every time they tried, Jesus had an answer for which there was no possible rebuttal. This served only to frustrate and infuriate them the more. These efforts were led by the Pharisees, but the Sadducees were also very much in support of the effort to stop this new teacher, and many times went along to watch.

The rising attitude of opposition to Jesus gave the three friends much cause for concern for their own selves as it became more and more impossible to bring up the positive aspects of Jesus's teaching and healings. The fever pitch of the Sanhedrin was at a level where almost all were seeking a way to put an end to Jesus, and any who would follow, or even speak of Him. It was almost dangerous to even speak his name.

Gamaliel was continually asking the members to keep calm in their discussions and meetings. There were also now meetings in secret between the High Priest and his personal friends, not open to the other members of the Grand Sanhedrin. It was never revealed what was said behind the closed doors of these meetings, but the hints, the questions, the accusatory remarks increased to a point to where Jesus went nowhere where there was not a member or representative of the Grand Sanhedrin close by, ready to find a flaw in His speaking or an action which could be interpreted as a breaking of the Mosaic Law, which then could be turned into a charge against Him. In all these attempts, over a period of almost two years, only frustration could be found as Jesus not only spoke the truth, but was always ready for those sent to entrap Him.

IT WAS AGAIN APPROACHING THE TIME for the great Feast of the Passover, the most important feast of the Hebrew nation, celebrating the freeing of the nation from slavery in Egypt and the beginning of the nation of Israel. Every year, many thousands of people made the trip to Jerusalem for the celebration. People all over the city were asking whether they thought Jesus of Nazareth would come for the great festival, but no one seemed to know for sure. Would he clear the money changers from the Temple square? Would he perform miracles in the city? Would He speak to people in a public gathering? Everyone seemed to be in great anticipation as the festival drew closer. No matter where the members of the Grand Sanhedrin went, they heard the name of Jesus being spoken.

Suddenly, a new report seemed to override all other stories being passed around. In Bethany, just a short distance from Jerusalem, a man named Lazarus had been raised from the grave after being dead for four days. There were small differences in the story, but the facts were clear. Jesus had called this man to come out from the grave where he had been laid. He had been prepared in the customary manner with spices and wrappings, but when he was called by Jesus, he emerged from the tomb—with the wrappings still tightly wound around him. Then Jesus told those close to "loose him and let him go". They gave him a robe and he walked away from the gravesite to the cheers and amazement of the people there. Jesus was again quickly not to be found.

When the three Pharisees came together, they were at a loss for words. "I know this man Lazarus," said Nicodemus.

"I also know him," joined Joseph. And Gamaliel added his similar comment. "He has worked on many synagogues close to Jerusalem, and his work is said to be excellent. I believe I have actually met this man and found him very open to our way of thought about Jesus and the Messiah. He lives with two sisters in Bethany. Perhaps we could plan a visit with them."

This last comment was met with mutual agreement and plans were made for the short trip to Bethany. But as the Passover was nearly upon them, they would have to wait for the celebration to end and the thousands of visitors to leave for their homes.

Gamaliel was going through his treasure trove of thoughts on Jesus and the Messiah, especially the words of the Prophet Isaiah, when another thought came into his mind—a thought that had been there for a good period of time, but one he had never focused on until the confirmation to him of this Jesus being the actual Son of God. As Gamaliel hurried to again meet with his two friends, his mind was filled with a blur of ideas that might be used to affect the Grand Sanhedrin. He would not be able to blatantly share what he knew because in the mood the council was in, there would be charges thrown at him and about him, and for not one moment did he think they would listen to what he had to say.

The Grand Sanhedrin was not in a normal reasoning mode. There were those who were constantly trying to agitate the others in order to get them to agree with their comments, each member trying to be heard above the rest. He must plan his words very carefully.

Gamaliel had already been the voice of calm in the midst of many meetings and he did not want to lose that ability in future discussions. He could hear the already agitated voices as he approached the meeting hall. As he came close to the entryway of the great meeting place of the Sanhedrin, the "Hall of Hewn Stone", Gamaliel took a deep breath and silently prayed to Jehovah asking for words of wisdom to use in this time of turmoil. Because of the respect of the Sanhedrin for Gamaliel as a man of great wisdom and training, the noise level seemed to drop and the group quieted further as Gamaliel moved toward the speaking stone, a raised pedestal in the center close to the front of the horseshoe-shaped room.

"Neighbors!"

Now the sound faded into silence as everyone there stopped to listen to the words this highly respected Pharisee would speak to them. "I also have heard the stories of this Jesus of Nazareth just as you have. But I ask you—does he speak against our father, Abraham? Has he taught against the Law as given by Moses? Have his disciples gathered against the laws of temple worship? Has any one of you found him in rebellion against the Romans? We have had other self-proclaimed leaders who have built a group of followers and they have come to nothing. What is it about this Jesus that has you so wroth? Perhaps we just need some more time to watch and wait to see how far this Jesus will go before we know his true intentions. He has done only good among our people. His teachings have been found within the Law. We need to not take our personal feelings against this Jesus out on one another. Please maintain our relationship in this great meeting hall at the highest level such that we can make proper decisions. I believe that we will find our answers in the writings of Isaiah the Prophet. I have been reading many words that match the signs we are witnessing today."

The room was filled with a soft murmuring as the whole meeting considered the wisdom of this advice. It would probably not last long, but for now there was a pause in the agitated arguing. The Grand Sanhedrin slowly turned to other items of business and the meeting went forward.

As the three friends later left the great hall of meeting, Nicodemus turned to the other two and said, "We must be very careful in our speaking and sharing of our belief on this matter, as the High Priest is against this Jesus, and speaking about Jesus is permissible only as long as the speaking protects the High Priest's position in the temple and his favor with the Roman government. This High Priest also has many supporters who will listen only to him. We, ourselves, must be very cautious about what we say to others as there are those who are becoming aware of the way we are thinking, and they could turn against us and try to charge us as well. I have heard the High Priest has now been having meetings to which we have not been invited. This gives me cause to worry that the whole purpose of the Sanhedrin may be ignored in order to satisfy the desires of the few. I see the focus on Jehovah being bypassed to satisfy the personal feelings of these radicals, who are the most outspoken and the loudest of all."

"We have only a few days before the Passover is here. We need to watch and pray for the will of Jehovah to come forth and be accomplished." This from Joseph, who though not always outspoken, was of deep, thoughtful, mannerisms.

The way through the city was almost impassable with so many people arriving for the great celebration of the Passover. Although the Pharisees were dressed in their robes depicting their high position, there was still a great amount of jostling and weaving among people to make their way. They listened as they slowly walked through the overcrowded way and realized that most of what they were hearing was talk about Jesus of Nazareth and whether or not He would come to Jerusalem and would He perform a miracle while in the city for all to see. The Pharisees sensed the rising excitement the name of Jesus was causing. The city was already in a state of turmoil with so many travelers from around the known world. Merchants from seemingly everywhere were setting up their booths or tents, shouting with all the others to be heard above the general level of sound in order to make a profit while they were in such a large gathering. It was difficult to even carry on a conversation while moving down the street.

The next day, they and their families gathered at the house of Gamaliel where they had agreed to eat the evening meal. Shortly after eating, Nicodemus excused himself from the discussion and left. He did not say where he was going, only that he would be back. The others wondered and talked about this, as Nicodemus was not one who kept quiet about what he was doing.

It was much later in the evening when Nicodemus returned and sat down without saying a word. The others, recognizing his deep, thoughtful mood, remained silent, waiting for him to speak.

"What is this *born of the spirit*?" were his first words. "How can a man be *born of water and the Spirit*?" He looked up as the other two looked at him expectantly. "These were the words that Jesus spoke to me when I talked to Him not long ago."

"You talked to Jesus?" asked Gamaliel in surprise.

"Yes. I heard where he was staying just outside the city and went there to see if I would have a chance to meet Him. He told me that in order to enter the kingdom of Heaven, I must be born of water and the Spirit. I understand the cleansing of water and the washing away of the old self, but I have not come to the full concept of being born of the Spirit. Does the Spirit of Jehovah actually wash us in order to be in the will of Jehovah? I have pondered this for many hours, discussing it with no one, but have now come to a place after speaking with Jesus where I need answers. Some nights I wake from my sleeping, remembering teaching from Hillel that spoke of this being born of the Spirit. What does the Spirit have to do with entering into the Kingdom of Heaven? I believe we need to be even more attentive to the teachings of this Rabbi, Jesus. If he truly is the Son of Jehovah, there may be some things we have missed in the concepts of our studies."

Joseph had been silent, listening to the words of Nicodemus, "I have been trying to gather everything I can from those who have heard Him or have followed Him long or even for a short while, but I confess I also do not understand this Spirit or where He fits in the plan of Jehovah. Gamaliel, you were so very close to your great-grandfather. Do you remember him ever speaking of this?"

Gamaliel was also deep in thought about this idea spoken by Nicodemus. "The Spirit of Jehovah is spoken of many times in the old writings, but not in the promise of Heaven. How does this fit with the words the mother of Jesus told me? She also spoke of the Spirit of Jehovah in the story of the birth of Jesus. I am beginning to believe that we should learn more about this Spirit of Jehovah as Hillel spoke freely about this often. I know that Jehovah has a Spirit, but I as yet do not have a full understanding of Him. I am trying to connect all of my thoughts about Jesus and learn more of this Spirit of Jehovah. Perhaps we could even speak with Jesus. If what we believe is true, and this Jesus is the true Son of Jehovah, then there is definitely a meaning we have not grasped as yet and need to learn more about."

With more questions than answers, the three separated for the day, knowing the next day would bring something new with stories of Jesus in almost every street and corner business in the city of Jerusalem. With all the responsibilities of their positions, and now the Passover upon them, they had still not—themselves as a group—personally heard Jesus speak. Most of His ministry was not in Jerusalem but in the northern part of Israel, especially the area of Galilee. Perhaps they would have that chance if He came to Jerusalem again for the Passover. The rest of the day was extremely busy with so many coming to the temple, asking questions in order to prepare properly for the celebration.

It was only the next morning when they were disturbed, while in the Temple, by sounds of a gathering a short distance away toward the Mount of Olives. Upon moving to a place where they could see the path going through the Mount, they saw a large crowd of people waving their arms with palm fronds and throwing their cloaks on the path in front of a small donkey with a rider on its back. The crowd grew larger as it neared the eastern gate of Jerusalem and the sound became stronger to those listening and observing from the steps leading to the Temple. Gamaliel, watching with his two friends and many others who were on the steps at that time, said to his two friends, "This I did not expect so soon. If this following grows any larger, the High Priest is going to have to confront this man and the crowd who is following Him. This will be seen as a direct challenge to the authority of those who sit in the high positions of our nation's leadership. Riding into the city on the donkey is a sign of royalty. I do not know what action the High Priest will take, but I do not believe it will be for the good."

"But what can we do?" asked Nicodemus. "We are but three and they have the numbers to overpower and actually ignore us. We are caught in the middle of all of this. We have already been left out of some of the meetings of the High Priest. It is obvious they have a plan or snare in place and are waiting to spring it. I do not know how they would try to charge Him at this time as this is the Passover, and no legal trial or action is allowed during these Holy days of celebration. I am fearful for Jesus, for I do not have great respect or trust in those who are our present leaders. It is possible they may find a way to go around the laws in order to try to end his teaching. The words of Jesus have not been spoken against our laws or against Jehovah, but they hate Him anyway. It is a madness they have against Him, and they will not listen nor rescind their attitudes."

Gamaliel said, "I agree with your words. I have also talked with those whom I thought were willing to listen to me, but they are caught up with the others on this path of believing this Rabbi is committing blasphemy. This last time the older Pharisees sent a newer member to challenge Him, but the new member was totally unprepared for the answer he was given and returned puzzled and feeling rebuked. This time, the words were brought to the three friends directly by a student who was close enough to hear clearly. He said that, 'If we would tear down the temple, He would rebuild it in three days.' This was the report the student gave." This brought a pause in the thinking and conversation of the three friends.

"This is something new that I am not aware of in all my studies. Perhaps there is a teaching we missed, forgot, or did not understand." Every time the words of Jesus came to the three Pharisees, they felt driven to return to the old studies of which they had been partaking most of their lives.

The next day, Gamaliel and Joseph were eating late in the morning when Nicodemus suddenly was beside them and spoke in hurried, hushed tones. "They arrested Him! They arrested Him."

"Who?" asked Gamaliel.

"Jesus!"

"When?" said Joseph.

"In the night—in the Garden of Gethsemane—the Temple guards came with a large group of other soldiers. They bound Him and led Him away under guard and scattered his disciples who were with Him. The Pharisees who were there were those the Chief Priest personally picked who he knew would do his bidding. This is what they have been hiding and plotting. They have completely ignored the law and proper procedure in their desire to do away with this teacher who has done nothing but good and spoken only what has been taught from the Law of Moses. We have been deliberately left out with many others of the Sanhedrin. This is a plot of only a few who would satisfy their own personal lusts and greed and mock Jehovah Himself in the process. Where is Jehovah's plan in all of this, for I cannot begin to put two thoughts together that fit what is now happening." He began to weep as he talked. "I have servants who are following to bring us news as soon as it is possible. I know not what we can or should do." He sat on the nearest bench and continued to weep as the shock of his words sank into their minds.

There was no sound from any of them except for the sound of weeping as the knowledge of what was happening went deep into their hearts. For a long period of time no one spoke, as each tried to understand how the Son of Jehovah could be treated in this manner. They continued in silence and tears for a very long period. Not a word was uttered as they waited for the next report from the servants of Nicodemus. Many times, servants were not paid attention to, and were allowed to get by a guard post when someone of higher level, like a student of a Pharisee, would be instantly noticed. This servant was well skilled in moving around in these kinds of meetings, as he had been with Nicodemus many times and was well acquainted with the Sanhedrin and many of the Roman soldiers also.

It was long into the night before any more news was brought, and then again only what the servants who had been joined by several others could hear from their appointed places. They were allowed to be only so close to the actual meeting area. The news was not at all in keeping with the rules normally followed by the Grand Sanhedrin. First of all, there were members of the Jerusalem Sanhedrin who were not on the Grand Sanhedrin but were avid supporters of the High Priest.

The first meeting to try Jesus took place in the courtyard of the High Priest's dwelling, a place where the High Priest was able to say who could and could not be allowed in the place where they were meeting and planning. The servants of Nicodemus were absolutely not allowed in that place. Then, very early in the morning, as the first meeting had been going on all night, the meeting moved to the palace of Pilate, who then saw fit to send Jesus to Herod who was also in Jerusalem to celebrate the Passover. After a short time there, the meeting moved back to the courtyard of Pilate where the loudest group was continually rousing everyone to create tumult until the Roman guards were called upon to try to still the disturbance. The loudest, being urged on by the servants of the High Priest, still continued to stir and instigate as they had been called upon to do by their masters, the High Priests. This group of instigators followed Jesus, his Roman soldier guards, the priests, and the rest of the noisemakers, back and forth between locations across the city causing sleep to hide from every house that was close to the pathway of the rioters.

Finally, Pilate was able to quiet the crowd and turned to Jesus. From where the servants were watching it seemed like Pilate was questioning Jesus. Then Pilate turned again to the crowd and, raising his hand for quiet, said, "I find no fault in this man."

The crowd began yelling and screaming again. Again, Pilate raised his hand calling for quiet.

Then Pilate gave them a choice of one of two prisoners they would want him to release—Jesus or a known criminal, Barabbas. (Barabbas, son of a former senior Pharisee who had served on the Grand Sanhedrin, had rebelled against the teaching of his father. He was named simply Barabbas by his criminal companions and also known to the authorities and the public as such. He was also suspected of insurrection and possibly even murder.) The noisy crowd not only cried for the release of Barabbas, but then went to the next level of crying for the crucifixion of Jesus, even though they did not and could not give a charge to use against Him. Finally, in order to gain control of the riot that was seemingly threatened, Pilate again called for quiet. Then, in the sight of everyone—people, priests, and Roman soldiers alike—he asked for a dish of water and washed his hands to symbolize that he would not be held responsible for anything that was done. He then released Barabbas and told the soldiers to crucify Jesus. This meant that the soldiers were given time to verbally and physically mistreat the prisoner before the punishment was carried out. With Jesus, this would have been especially harsh because of the claims of kingship attributed to Him. He would then be made to carry the crossbar of the cross to the hill called Golgotha, (Place of the Skull), where the prisoner to be crucified would be thrown on the ground and nailed to the wooden crossbar of the cross. Then the crossbar would be lifted up and attached to the pole which was already standing there waiting for the next victim. The pole was stained with the blood of those who had gone before. The number of people whose blood mingled and had soaked into the ground at that place could never be counted, but now there was one more victim's blood to be added—that of Jesus, the son of Jehovah, Himself.

After hearing the end of the report from the servant, the three Pharisees, who had lost the capacity to even speak, separated to go, each to their own homes to get some rest, as they had not been in a mental state where rest was possible. They had become too exhausted to do anything else. There was nothing they could do to change what was going to happen. Only the direct intervention of Jehovah Himself could stop the actions that had been set in place. Jehovah's Son was going to die by crucifixion on a Roman cross!

Gamaliel laid down only for a short time on his mat as sleep would not even come close while his mind was filled to overflowing with visions that were coming to him from the things he had seen of crucifixions carried out by the Romans. There was nothing pleasant about watching while passing by or even being within hearing distance when a man was dying on a cross.

The visions left nothing out, and he was not able to blot out the memories. He had watched as a condemned man had struggled to stand after being beaten by the Roman soldiers, only to be given the heavy crossbar of the cross to carry to the place where the cross was waiting.

The cross was already standing in a public place, often on a well-traveled road, so everyone would see and be warned not to go against the laws the Romans had written. The main upright portion of the cross had always been left for another after each death. The crossbar was thrown upon the ground and the victim was laid on it with the victim's arms stretched open and the nails driven through the hands. The crossbar with the victim nailed to it was then dragged upward along the upright post until the victim was hanging above ground. Next, the executioner would cross the feet, driving a long spike through both into the post. Thus there was pain from hanging and also pain from pushing up with the feet. This was the cruelest form of punishment man had ever used. He had no desire to see it again, especially with the belief that this was actually the "Son of Jehovah". If the victim did not die quickly enough, a spear was driven through the body.

But wait; if this was the Son of God, how was it possible for Him to be treated in this way? If Jehovah was God, how was it possible for man to even physically control His Son?

Gamaliel began to realize that Jehovah had to be allowing this crucifixion. Jehovah saw all that man was doing. What could possibly be the purpose of allowing your own son to die? How could Jehovah allow this great tragedy to take place?

Gamaliel then remembered the old statement. "He was led like a lamb to the slaughter." Was this what it meant? How could this be the way that God would save His people? Could the death of His own Son be the salvation of the people of God? Sleep finally came to the man known as a man of wisdom, but who knew that he was still weak in the ways of the Great God, Jehovah, who he had sought to serve his entire life.

BUT THEN, CLOSE TO MID-DAY, the three men were awakened from their exhausted state by their servants beating loudly on doors, calling for them to awaken and hasten to the outside to see what was happening. As they rushed into the open air, they were aware of wailing, crying, low moaning, and soft fearful screaming. As they stepped from their homes, they could see that the day was not right. In fact, there was no day. There was no light. The sun was nowhere to be seen in the sky. All was darkness as the deepest night. People were carrying torches and candles in what was supposed to be the brightest part of the day.

As they gathered together, Gamaliel spoke in a hushed tone, "It is Jehovah! He is speaking to us and showing us His displeasure. This sinful people have gone too far. I shake in fear for what He has planned for us next."

Just at that time they heard cries and screams from the Temple area and turned to try to safely make their way toward the sounds. As they grew closer to the great steps leading up to the doorway of the temple, they met priests running away from the Holy section of the Temple. Getting one of the priests to stop for a moment, they asked him why he was running away.

"The Veil in the Holy Place has been torn. The Ark of the Covenant is revealed to all and we are dead men, for no one can look upon the face of Jehovah and live," he gasped in a breathless voice. "I have to hide somewhere from his terrible wrath." He then turned quickly and again began running, stumbling in the darkness.

Gamaliel said to his two friends who had joined him. "Where do you hide from Jehovah?"

Joseph shook his head and answered, "Nowhere. There is nowhere you will be able to hide from His sight. We can only stand here and wait for Him to do what He will do next. Our sins? They are blatant before Him. We have just been part of the greatest sin ever known. We have hung Jehovah's own Son on the tree."

As they stood there, they began noticing that they could again begin to see. There was the beginning of light glowing from the sky and it was like the morning was just starting over and the light slowly grew as new as the new day. The three stood there, still and silent as the day became normal, until it became as if the day had not been interrupted.

"He is gone," said Gamaliel. " Jesus, the Messiah, the Son of Jehovah, is dead. We will meet on the morrow and study to see if the old thoughts and writings will give us clearness to what we have just been witness to." Gamaliel turned with the others and slowly began to go home.

Joseph suddenly stopped with Nicodemus beside him. "There is one thing I can yet do for this Jesus that will need to be done. I have a new tomb I just had recently carved close to this area that has yet to be used. It was carved for my own use when it is my time to die. We can place his body there. I will be honored to give it for His burial. I know I will be able to gain the ear of Pilate as my family has often done business with the Romans."

Nicodemus said, "I will bring spices, and servants to carry the body and the spices, but we do not have time to prepare the body properly before the Sabbath starts."

Joseph looked at his longtime friend, laying his hand upon his shoulder and thanking him, saying, "We will just have to do what we are able and wrap Him in a sheet with spices until the Sabbath is over, and then come and complete the wrapping with the women helping. That is all we can do at this time."

Joseph left to obtain his time with Pilate, and Nicodemus turned toward his home to prepare and direct his servants in his part of the gruesome task of readying a body for burial. This was to be one of the most difficult challenges of his life. This was not just a body. This was the Son of Jehovah, and now Nicodemus also knew Him from their short meeting.

Joseph was known to the guards at the palace of Pilate because of his status as a businessman in the city and was granted a hearing quickly because of the reason he came to see Pilate. He was granted permission to receive the body of Jesus, and going to the cross, he—with Nicodemus and their servants—gently removed the body of Jesus, wrapping it and carrying the body to the tomb of Joseph. There with the aid of the servants, they cleaned and wrapped the body and laid it on the stone bench prepared for that purpose, covering the face of Jesus with a clean, expensive cloth. Then using levers, the many servants of Joseph and Nicodemus rolled the great stone, cut for that purpose, into place, sealing the tomb. This task took the efforts of all of them, as the stone was of great size. They left slowly and silently, heading toward their homes to finish their own preparations for the Passover and the Sabbath.

The Passover was celebrated by all Hebrews, as this was the highest celebration of Israel, remembering the time that Jehovah had delivered them long ago from slavery in Egypt, bringing them out with a mighty hand and signs for all to see. But in Jerusalem, there seemed to be an unusual sense of tension.

The celebration was subdued by something that could not be totally explained. It was in the air, on people's faces, and in their conversations, which were done many places in hushed tones as if someone was listening, keeping a record of all the words used. In the homes of Gamaliel, Nicodemus, and Joseph, there was a special sadness and a mourning which was not the normal celebrative presence of mind those around them had come to expect.

Gamaliel had gone on several long walks by himself to be alone and to talk with Jehovah. His mind was overwhelmed by the questions about what had taken place with Jesus. His one focus was how Jehovah could promise over hundreds of years that He would send a deliverer, and then when He did in the form of His own Son, allow that deliverer, His only Son, to be treated in this way, even to be crucified. Gamaliel was not able to put it all together in a way that was understandable. Worse than that, how could it be possible the leaders of the Jewish nation would refuse to recognize the Messiah and take part in the most heinous crime to ever be committed? Gamaliel's mind and heart struggled over and over again for two days, accompanied by times of head pain and sickness such that he was not able to eat meals or taste food. Water was the only thing he was able to force into his tortured body. For two days, sleep was also unable to be grasped, as he could only sit and pray and wait for Jehovah's words to come.

Late in the morning, on the first day of the week, there was a strong knocking at the home of Gamaliel, from his servant. "Master, Master, come quickly. There is news." As Gamaliel opened the door, the servant rushed in with unseemly protocol, pushing the door open in his haste to get his message spoken.

"Please! Please! Calm yourself," said Gamaliel.

The servant continued as if he hadn't heard. "The tomb is empty! His body is gone! The guards are gone! The huge stone was rolled back to its place where it sat waiting to be used! What has happened? What has happened? What is happening?" A shocked silence descended on the room while those present tried to come up with an answer.

It was only a very short time later that Nicodemus and Joseph also arrived at the door of Gamaliel. They also had been given the news, as the students of the three were close and what was shared by one was shared by all. Entering the house of Gamaliel, they looked for a few seconds at each other and then began to sing Psalms of praise and worship—as they had been of like mind for years. The understanding of this happening opened their minds and confirmed their thoughts as taught them by Hillel the Elder many years before.

The servants joined in, as they had also heard and had learned along with the students. Gamaliel took advantage of this gathering and shared to all who were there the things Hillel the Elder had taught him from the time of his childhood.

Suddenly, everything that they had put in their minds and hearts came rushing together, and the praise now begun went all the way through the noon meal time. Old scriptures came into their minds as everyone became aware of the meaning and significance of phrases that before had not been totally understood.

Later, after finally taking time for a meal, the three friends sat down with all the students and servants who were gathered with them to contemplate what actions they should next be looking forward to in light of what the nation of Israel was experiencing at the news of the empty tomb. The news had spread like a fire in a pile of dry hay. The Healer had disappeared from His grave and there were now stories about him being seen alive and well.

There was another thing that was being made known by many people, and that was that many people had been seen walking around in the city of Jerusalem, saying they were from times long past with names that were remembered and recognized by many of the descendants of those very people. In fact, the graves of those who appeared healthy and walking around, had been opened by some strange unknown power, and people were in fear and disbelief over all this. Who had opened the graves and brought them back to life? Some of these walking through the streets were hundreds of years old and known only by stories handed down by the family history.

Where to focus their minds and hearts? These three men were not only teachers of the laws of the nation but were avid students of history and believed that the old and historical writings of the nation of Israel would hold the answers.

The news that Jesus had been seen alive and well was spreading like a great fire going over all Jerusalem. At the same time, they were trying to keep up with the current happenings of not only this Jesus, who had come out from the tomb, but his followers, who were now starting to say they had seen Him.

The three called their students together and built three teams of the brightest students and sent them out to follow and learn all there was to learn. As the word came that the followers of Jesus had moved to Galilee, one team was sent there to follow as closely as possible. One team remained in Jerusalem to gather information about the tomb and how this all happened. The third team, through their friends who were students of other Pharisees and Sadducees, would keep track of the actions of the local and Grand Sanhedrins, secret or otherwise, especially where the three were not invited.

The reports from the teams came back with multiple stories and descriptions; Jesus had been seen with His disciples many times in Galilee, and once by a group of hundreds of people, but never in one place very long. The three Pharisees kept track of everything they could and realized they were just waiting for the next sign from Jehovah. Then the reports stopped as if Jesus had again gone away somewhere, and did not appear again.

Then suddenly, the focus moved back to Jerusalem as the

followers of Jesus, now being called, "The Way", came back to the city and were meeting together in one of the larger rooms of the temple. They were spending every day in prayer together, men and women alike, going long into the night. The crowds were growing larger. As the crowds grew, the Sanhedrin became more and more perplexed, as they had little or no control over the situation. Many of the Pharisees and Sadducees kept to themselves and hid in their homes, as they had no answers to satisfy those who were seeking. At the same time, many others had joined the groups following the teachings of Jesus. The city was divided.

In their meetings together, the three Pharisees with their students and servants, (for they also taught the servants when they wished to learn), the discussion was primarily on what they could expect and how to prepare for it. As the next large festival was the Feast of Weeks, they turned their attention to that time fast arriving. Jehovah had given them festivals to remember Him by, and the Feast of Weeks was celebrated after the barley harvest and was a time of praise for Jehovah's goodness to Israel for the abundance of the crop and a time for sharing with others. With great anticipation, they looked forward to what Jehovah had prepared for them.

Then, the sign came, but in a new way. While in the meeting of the followers of "The Way" who were still praying and praising Jehovah, there was heard the sound of a strong wind which entered the room where this group had gathered and brought with it the appearance of tongues of fire which settled on the heads of all those who were there. This wind was heard over a large section of Jerusalem. Those in the room began speaking in languages they had not known before. There were many varied descriptions of what was taking place by the people gathering outside trying to see what was happening, but there were people of many languages from many lands outside of the gathering and they were each hearing the message about Jesus being spoken in their own dialect. That had not been a part of the meetings before this. In fact, the languages being spoken were spoken by those who had knowledge of only two or three languages before the arrival of this wind. There was no answer as to where the tongues came from on this day. Each person who had been touched by a flaming tongue spoke a different language. The news of what was happening spread throughout the city of Jerusalem. The news also started to spread through the whole country as the visitors in Jerusalem left for their homes.

When the three friends again met, each bringing their thoughts as to what this could mean, Gamaliel spoke first. "I have an explanation for this," he said. "I believe the wind that was heard may actually be the actual breath of Jehovah, even perhaps His Holy Spirit. Jehovah is breathing life into this world, even after we tried to murder His Son. This is the greatest sign of Jehovah's love He could ever give. No higher power could ever love like this. Only Jehovah could love a people who had just hung His Son on the cross."

THE ENTIRE GRAND SANHEDRIN had become in total disarray. The stories of Jesus being gone from the tomb wherein his body had lain for three days spread wildly across Jerusalem and the entire nation. Now this new happening was added to the story of Jesus being told and quickly spread across all Israel. The story was not spread by just one, but now by hundreds of people from all levels of Jewish society, from the very rich to the very poor. The three Pharisees tried to speak in the meetings of the Grand Sanhedrin defending the new movement, but were shouted down every time they tried to speak. Joseph and Nicodemus became known as ones who were part of the new teachings, and when it also became common knowledge that they had taken the body of Jesus and had cared for it, even using Joseph's tomb, they were ostracized by the Grand Sanhedrin and not allowed to speak in any meeting; even greetings from another neighbor were becoming sparse.

Saul, from Tarsus, one of the newer members, became more and more outspoken against anything that had to do with even the mention of the name of Jesus, and began to build a following against "The Way". This group now was moving to threats of personal violence toward anyone who was connected to "The Way" or even speaking of it. This of course was absolutely oppositional to the way the Grand Sanhedrin was supposed to present themselves to the people of the nation.

As the Grand Sanhedrin could not find a way to control the spread of the news of "The Way", in their lost confusion, the fiery words of Saul brought many of them to support his angry attitude. The Grand Sanhedrin was beginning to split, as there were others who were coming to believe the truth about Jesus, but the majority refused to give up on the old way of thinking. Saul became more and more fiery and outspoken, even interrupting and speaking over another neighbor when they were speaking. He actually went to the high priest where he asked for and received a letter of approval, allowing him to arrest and put in chains any who would not recant their beliefs about Jesus. This letter also gave him authority to pursue any believers to other locations and arrest them there. It was on one of these trips that Saul actually met Jesus, on the road to Damascus, in Syria.

GAMALIEL, JOSEPH, AND NICODEMUS talked long and came to the decision that they should find and meet with the original close followers of Jesus. They left the room where they were meeting and made their way through the city streets to where they had been told they would find the disciples. They did not have to look very long as the Grand Sanhedrin was keeping the disciples watched so as to find a way to accuse them further. As more of the Grand Sanhedrin began to become part of "The Way", the number of empty seats in the great meeting room was growing. It was therefore a simple task to find out where the disciples were meeting.

The three men went to where they had been told and found many of the disciples of Jesus there. When the three Pharisees joined the group, there were raised eyebrows, but also a warm welcome from the disciples. Many of the disciples knew that these three had become part of "The Way". Gamaliel was well known to many by sight because of the wisdom he had demonstrated in positions of leadership and his ever wandering visits to the center of activity in the city. He was also known as the great-grandson of Hillel the Elder, one of the wisest in the history of Israel. When the three entered the room, a silence came over all those who were there.

As the members of the disciples waited to find the purpose for the visit of the three Pharisees, Gamaliel gave introductions and spoke for the three and explained that they wanted to know more of Jesus. He also told them they had been long ago trained by Hillel the Elder to be looking for and expecting Jesus to appear, for the time and the signs were close.

This statement opened the door to newfound thoughts, and conversation began. For the rest of the evening there was a time of getting to know one another between the disciples and Pharisees, and the time of sharing went very late as there was more to be said than ever could be shared in one evening. It was long into morning hours before they gave up for the night.

This was the first of many hours of the three sharing time with members of those who walked with Jesus. Because the three Pharisees had received most of their information second hand from the street and their servants, they were eager to learn from those who had been closest to Jesus and had personal knowledge of His teaching. Sometimes the wording was a bit different, but the stories they told were agreed upon by all. The Pharisees, because of their years of training, instantly understood the messages Jesus had given to people were connected to the old Mosaic laws, the law the three Pharisees understood. It all came into an understanding they had never before totally realized. Jesus fulfilled every requirement of the Mosaic Law and then made the law plain for everyone to see. The three Pharisees, when together, said to one another, "How could we not have seen this before?" Each day they learned more of what Jesus had said and done.

One evening the Pharisees turned the subject to the disciples themselves. Gamaliel led with the question, "I hear Galilee in your voices and would like to hear how you all came to be part of the Son of Jehovah and His teaching."

For a few seconds there was silence as the disciples thought back to when they had met Jesus. Then the man called Andrew spoke. "My brother and I had become followers of 'John the Baptizer' who spoke often that he was here to announce the one chosen by Jehovah to bring Israel back to the worship of Jehovah. It was this same John who pointed out Jesus to us, and we then began to listen to this new teacher, Jesus, who spoke in a different way. Every word he spoke seemed to be filled with love, and there was a sense of peace about Him that we could not describe. Our hearts began to fill with a new love for Jehovah we had never known before. We did not want to leave His side. It was Jesus who told us He was the Son of Jehovah."

Gamaliel shared about the teaching of Hillel the Elder, who as his great-grandfather, had trained him from the time of his very young childhood about Jehovah sending His own Son. He then spoke of how he had actually gone to Nazareth and spoken to Mary, the mother of Jesus, and had been told by her of the birth of Jesus and the events surrounding that night. The Pharisees listened as the story of Jesus became more complete and their teachings were being fulfilled.

One called Matthew told how he had been a very young tax collector in Bethlehem at the time of the birth of Jesus and had seen Him as a very young child in the home of Joseph and Mary. He knew them only a short time, as the family disappeared in the night, right after a very large caravan from the East had come to visit. He did not know where they went. They were just gone.

This was at the time when Herod ordered all the boys under two years of age to be killed. Herod died shortly after that time, but Matthew did not again know of Jesus until He began teaching in Galilee. Even then, it was only after he had been called by Jesus to join Him before it all came together that this was the same Jesus he had known as a child in Bethlehem.

Then one called Simon spoke and told how Jesus had invited him to leave a life of anger and violence as a Zealot to become part of a life of love and peace. "I do not understand how Jesus could choose me as I had so much in my life to be forgiven. But as we walked together, the peace He offered became a part of my life and I am not who I was. I am just beginning to understand—as I share with others—the true meaning of this peace, and I will never go back to what I was."

Then one who looked very young spoke. "My father, Zebedee, taught our family while we were very young to be always looking forward to the time when the Messiah would come to bring His people back to a right-standing relationship with Jehovah. Even then, I was not ready when Jesus called my brother and I to walk with Him. My father was willing for me to go only because James, my older brother, had also been called to go with Jesus. Our father, Zebedee the fisherman, was one who believed also that the Messiah was to come very soon, and so is one of those who understands the things that we have been witness of during our time with the Master. There were many days as a child of talking about the promise of Jehovah while fishing out on the Sea of Galilee, and I was early hearing about the coming of the Messiah, the "Anointed One". Jesus, our Master, took me under His wing and was like a father to me as I had left home at a young age. The teaching and beliefs of our father prepared us well for the things we now know as truth. I hope to be able to write down the truths I have heard and witnessed for others to also understand in their hearts who Jesus is and why He has come."

There was a short pause as the others were thinking about what they would add when one called Thomas began speaking in a quiet voice. "I was raised in a family who developed a trading business and was taught to seek truth in everything I was told. I needed to have proof for everything. I was always careful to examine all things before accepting them as truth. But when Jesus came into the room that day and asked me to put my hands into the wounds He had suffered on the cross, there remained no longer any question in me. Jesus is the Son of Jehovah, our Messiah. Now I am filled with desire to share with everyone the truth, so they may also have the joy that has been imparted to my heart and soul and will never leave. I have been thinking about going with one of my family's trade caravans myself, and share the news of Jesus with far away people who may not have heard."

One after another, the disciples gathered in the room answered in like fashion, each being called to a new life and leaving behind all they had to go and learn from Jesus the new way of living life under the love of Jehovah. Now they were being sent out to share this Good News with all who would listen, and then themselves spread the news to others.

As Joseph talked about spending more and more time among the followers of Jesus, he began to feel in his heart that he should also go out into the world, as Jesus had commanded his disciples, to go to places other than Israel, further away. He, after a time, chose to take one of the trade ships of the business his family had developed, and after offering the use of his family's ships and caravans for the disciples to travel with, left himself, to travel across the Great Sea to the West to share the message of Jesus, leaving his beloved homeland. It is said he arrived in what is now Wales of the British Isles, where he began sharing the story of Jesus, His message, and the fact that He had risen from the tomb. (Glastonbury Abbey, said to be of the work of Joseph of Arimathea, is still there today).

Nicodemus was called to give an account of his actions before the Grand Sanhedrin and the High Priest. He did not back down, but told the entire body of the Grand Sanhedrin of helping to prepare and place the body of Jesus in the tomb, and that Jesus was truly dead at the time of burial. He was asked to explain the empty tomb but would only say that this was the work of Jehovah himself and that Jesus must have truly been the Son of Jehovah for this to happen. The Grand Sanhedrin began yelling "blasphemy", and tearing their robes, threw him out of the meeting room and off the high council, and even told him to leave Jerusalem or he would be stoned in public. Nicodemus went back to his home town and there finding a small group of believers in "The Way" began teaching and spreading the news of Jesus to all who would listen. He continued in this way the rest of his life, going to whoever would receive him and listen to the news of Jesus he had to share.

Gamaliel was also called to give an answer for his beliefs and actions, but because of the high respect for his wisdom and the tradition handed down by his great-grandfather, Hillel the Elder, he was treated with more dignity. He said, "What I have learned and taught are the words of my great-grandfather, and the words given by Jehovah. Nowhere in my teachings have I ever spoken against the Law of Moses or the wisdom of our fathers. If anyone has heard me do so, they may lay out and bring forth the charges against me to this body at this time. No one has proven the words of this Jesus to be not true. If anyone here can do so, speak now in front of these witnesses so that all may hear. This great council has been in place to lead this nation for many years, and has had many disagreements. We must continue to take great care that our decisions are correct and just before Jehovah."

The demeanor of Gamaliel never wavered as he spoke as one of authority, and his words came as of great wisdom. He was not threatened or thrown out of the meeting, but many turned away from listening to his speaking and eventually he left the Grand Sanhedrin. Many, because of the speaking of Gamaliel, began to search out his words and became part of "The Way", because they knew that Gamaliel had never spoken without great thought and meditation.

Many, after coming to Gamaliel and listening again to his words, were persuaded in their hearts that Jesus was indeed the Son of Jehovah, and was the promised Messiah. They joyfully joined the other believers who were growing rapidly in number all over Israel.

Gamaliel left the presence of the Grand Sanhedrin, and as he had been taught by his great-grandfather, went out among the people of the city and shared the message of Jesus. He located the groups of followers of Jesus, who had now become known as "The Way". Learning of all Jesus had taught, he began teaching, going about all of Israel, teaching about Jesus being the actual Son of Jehovah and about the love in the promise of the Old Mosaic Law and its promise being fulfilled in the coming of Jesus as the promised Messiah, the Son of God.

Gamaliel lived till 56 A.D. and died knowing the things his

great-grandfather had shared were indeed the truth. Jesus was the "Son of God" and the Messiah sent to restore Israel to the relationship with the Creator God, known as "Jehovah".

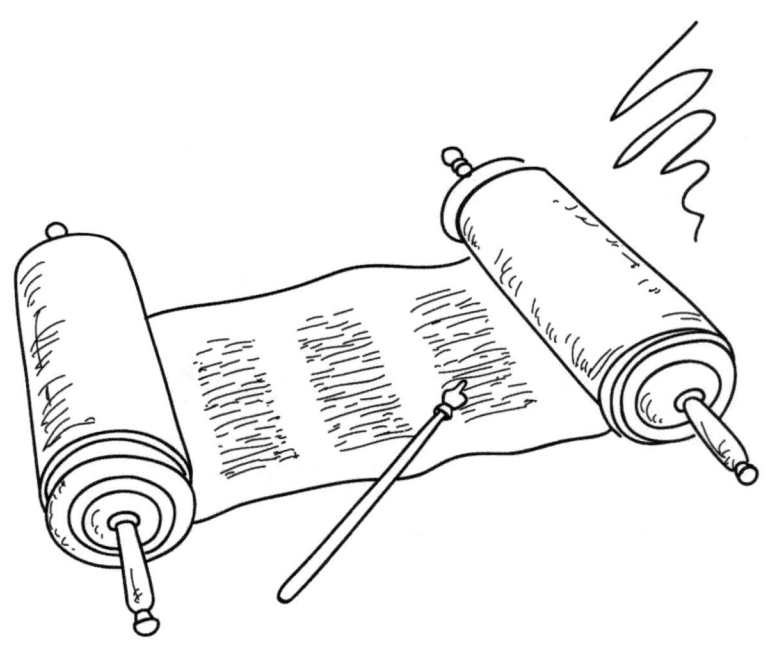

## One Man

As I have read the Bible through my many years of life, I have always been fascinated by the fact that Jehovah, God, has always maintained a remnant of those who believe in Jehovah, upon which He builds again and again after each failure of man. This rebuilding is the truth of God's ultimate love for His creation. That remnant needs not to be large—in fact, it may only be one man, such as Noah, that God uses.

Who was that remnant who carried forth the seed of truth preparing for the "Anointed One", the "Messiah"?

This story is just a bit about one man who studied the history, and the law and writings of his people, called "Hebrews", and began to understand the desire of Jehovah and the true meaning of love in the rules Jehovah had designed for them to follow. As this man—"Hillel the Elder"—realized the importance of his findings, he decided to share them with his great-grandson for the continuance of the remnant and the belief that Jehovah was a God of infinite love.

If just one man believes in the truth and shares that belief, many others may also become a part of the remnant.

## Author's Note

The love in the Mosaic Law is still true today and is shared in the New Testament of the Bible. The promise of God is for all without exception. If you would like to be part of the promise of eternity, below is the way.

### The Problem
Romans 3:23

All have sinned and fall short of the glory of God

### The Consequence
Romans 6:23

The wages of sin is death, but the free gift of God is eternal life in Jesus Christ, our Lord

### The Solution, He Paid Our Penalty
Romans 5:8

While we were yet sinners, Jesus Christ died for us

### The Response
Romans 10:9-10

If you confess with your mouth that Jesus Christ is Lord, and believe in your heart that God raised Him from the dead, you will be saved

### The Assurance
Romans 10:13

Whoever will call on the name of the Lord will be saved

(Above scripture references on this page are from the New American Standard Bible)

## Why I Write

I have always treasured the many stories of the Bible, and as a lifelong student of its Word, I have yearned for detail, for images of what happened in the moments before or after an event that is recorded within its holy pages. My books are an attempt to put into words what my study has revealed to my mind and heart.

## With Gratitude

As I offer this short book for others to read, I want to thank Mary, my wife, for her love, her patience, and her input. Her concepts of God's word have added greatly to our lives and our walk with the Lord, Jesus.

# ALSO BY
# CHARLES G. DORSEY

**NOT ALONE**
*The Birth That Changed The World*

www.ingramcontent.com/pod-product-compliance
Lightning Source LLC
Chambersburg PA
CBHW061453040426
42450CB00007B/1346